~ Over Easy ~
~ Cracking the Shell ~

By Olivia Valency

ISBN: 979-8-9946200-5-2

Any mention of Calvinism is specific to the church where I grew up and how I recall it being taught to me by my mother, teachers, and preachers throughout my life. It's not always taught the same way in all Calvinist churches. Calvin never used the phrase fast-forward video. I use that phrase so that my readers can get a better understanding of Calvin's doctrine. All scripture is quoted from the King James Version Bible unless noted otherwise.

For privacy reasons, some names, locations, and dates may have been changed.

First edition, March 2026

Books written by Olivia Valency

Scrambled Eggs ~ Walking on Shells

Sunny Side Up ~ Eggshells to Seashells

Deviled Eggs ~ Shells in the Yolk

Poached Eggs ~ Selling Empty Shells

Over Easy ~ Cracking the Shell

Special thanks to my daughters,
Hannah and Heather,
for proofreading and editing.

TABLE OF CONTENTS

~ Fried Apples ~ 1

~ Applesauce ~ 5

~ Apple Pie in the Sky ~ 12

~ An Apple Per Day ~ 16

~ The Big Apple ~ 25

~ Apples and Worms ~ 36

~ Rotten to the Core ~ 47

~ The Apple Tree ~ 55

~ One Bad Apple ~ 64

~ Apple of His Eye ~ 79

~ Poisoned Apples ~ 88

~ Apple-y Ever After ~ 98

~ Little Buddy ~ 103

~ Fried Apples ~

Disclaimer: This book might fry your apple or at least make your head spin. Read at your own risk! John Calvin didn't use the words "fast-forward video." I use that phrase only to help my readers better understand Calvinism. That being said, let's take a big ol' juicy bite out of John Calvin's apple.

In the early 1500s, John Calvin interpreted the Bible. He presented many confusing and contradictory opinions, views, and ideas. He developed his predestination-only and no-free-will doctrine, which is now known as the theology of Calvinism.

Predestination means: to foreordain, predetermine, or mark out beforehand. It also means to destine someone for a specific fate or purpose, or to determine an outcome or course of events in advance by divine will or fate.

Even though it's not defined as such in the Bible, Calvin interpreted predestination to mean that, before God created the earth or any people whatsoever, He used His divine foresight and watched trillions of hours of fast-forward videos that revealed everyone's entire future.

John Calvin asserted that God has complete foreknowledge of everyone's thoughts, actions, and words throughout their entire life. He also said that God saw Judgment Day and has already decided who will go to heaven or hell. Calvin understood this foreknowledge to mean that Father had already pre-judged and predestined everyone's life and destiny.

Calvin claimed that God used passive action to foresee all future events and then used active action to solidify them as unchangeable. He said that no one can deviate from what God foresaw, so now, nobody has free will. He stated that God predestined everyone to perform their real life as a replica of their fast-forward video. By combining his two separate opinions, Calvin created his predestination-only and no-free-will doctrine.

Calvin twisted the words foresight and predestined together. He used these two terms interchangeably, implying they mean the same thing. However, they are not the same word, nor do they have the same meaning. One is apples, and the other is oranges. Passive foresight is not the same as taking direct action. Observing passively is different from forcing people toward a destiny. We can't say that God's alleged foreseeing is identical to God's predestining people to their fate.

Calvin states that, based on God's foresight, He chose a select few outstanding people and gave them special tasks and a golden ticket to heaven. He explains that these are God's predestined elect. He also said that God will cast most people into hell as punishment for their alleged foreseen evil deeds. Calvin depicts God as simply sitting on His throne and watching the play-by-play, real-life version unfold.

Besides Satan and his evil angels, the Bible doesn't say that God has condemned anyone to hell. Instead, it emphasizes that God wants everyone to repent and be saved, showing that God loves all His children and that we all have free will to choose salvation.

Calvin portrayed God as a puppet master, with us as the puppets acting out God's foreseen mental movie. If our loving Father knew all future events, He would send prophets, preachers, and teachers to prevent most of His children from ending up in an eternal smoker.

Satan twists scripture to deceive people, and John Calvin also manipulated scripture to match his opinions. Calvin imposed his fast-forward video and no-free-will narrative onto the scriptures. If God knew everyone's destiny, He would not have created evil people. He would not have sent prophets and preachers. If God knew who would go to heaven, He wouldn't have created flesh bodies when a much better spiritual body exists.

"It is sown a natural body; it is raised a spiritual body. There is a natural body, and there is a spiritual body. And as we have borne the image of the earthy, we shall also bear the image of the heavenly. Now this I say, brethren, that flesh and blood cannot inherit the kingdom of God" (1 Cor 15:44, 49, 50).

When I was young, I asked, "If God already knows our final destination, why do we even have to live here on earth? Why didn't God just create everyone and place them directly in heaven or hell? Why didn't He just skip the real-life version?" I was told that it wouldn't be fair to throw people into hell unless they actually committed what God foresaw in their video.

Calvin used the term Divine Sovereignty to define omnipotence as God being all-powerful. However, he claimed that because God possesses ultimate power, it also means God watches fast-forward videos and predestines everything to happen exactly as He foresaw, resulting in nobody having any free will.

Omnipotent: A biblical term that describes God as all-powerful and having infinite power and authority.

Omnipresent: A word not in the Bible, but used by theologians to portray God as being present everywhere all at the same time.

Omniscient: A term not in the Bible, but used by scholars to describe God as all-knowing — in a state of knowing everything.

John Calvin interpreted omniscience as God's knowledge of everything that is happening now, has happened in the past, and will happen in the future, including everyone's final destiny and afterlife.

The Bible does not say God has foreknowledge of all future actions and destinies. It also doesn't say that nobody has free will. Even though there's no biblical proof for these ideas, they are Calvin's two main beliefs that form the core of his doctrine. He built his entire religious theology on these two opinions. How do you like those crazy apples?

~ Applesauce ~

Calvin teaches that nobody can choose eternal life. His teaching that God predestined everyone to either heaven or hell contradicts Jesus' teachings. The Bible clearly states that whosoever believes in Jesus shall have eternal life. Jesus said that salvation is available to anyone who embraces it and turns their heart to loving our Father.

"For God so loved the world, that he gave his only begotten Son, that whosoever believeth in him should not perish, but have everlasting life" (Jn 3:16).

Calvin teaches that only God's elect can believe in Jesus because that's what God saw them doing in their video. Calvin says the vast majority of people cannot embrace salvation because God saw they rejected Him during their video.

The Bible states that God predestined certain people to carry out specific tasks for Him. One example is:

"Before I formed thee in the belly I knew thee; and before thou camest forth out of the womb I sanctified thee, and I ordained thee a prophet unto the nations" (Jer 1:5).

> And we know that all things work together for good to them that love God, to them who are the called according to his purpose. For whom he did foreknow, he also did predestinate to be conformed to the image of his Son, that he might be the firstborn among many brethren. Moreover whom he did predestinate, them he also called: and whom he called, them he also justified: and whom he justified, them he also glorified. (Rom 8:28-30)

Calvin understood that before Jeremiah's earthly life, God saw that he was a good and trustworthy man who loved Him. Calvin concluded that since God predestined Jeremiah before he was born, then, to be fair, God must have predestined everyone beforehand. I'm sure Calvin took a few bites of his apple as he pondered how it was fair for God to predestine Jeremiah as a prophet and to have previously justified and judged him as righteous — and not someone else.

Calvin willfully ignored and neglected to consider all the possibilities of how God knew Jeremiah. Calvin, believing it was impossible and closing his mind, rejected the idea that Jeremiah physically existed and literally proved himself before being born in the flesh.

We know that existence before the womb is possible. Jesus existed before coming to earth. Father predestined and judged Jesus as righteous before entering Mary's womb:

"In the beginning was the Word, and the Word was with God, and the Word was God. And the Word was made flesh, and dwelt among us" (Jn 1:1, 14).

God is the Word. Father has no beginning or end. The Word became flesh. Jesus lived among us.

Calvin altered Jeremiah 1:5 to say, "Before you entered your mother's womb, I saw a fast-forward video, which showed me you were worthy to go to heaven, so I predestined you to be a prophet here in your real-life version."

If God had foresight of how everything would unfold, He wouldn't need to predestine anything differently. He would simply let everyone's real-life play out exactly as He observed, and all would be well. Calvin depicts God as going overboard, suggesting that God actively predestined all real-life versions to remain the same and not deviate from the videos.

Calvin assigned many meanings to the word predestined. He was trying to force a square peg into a round hole.

Calvin first expressed his view that predestination means God foresaw everyone's entire life actions and afterlife destiny through mental fast-forward videos before anyone entered their mother's womb.

Calvin also interpreted predestination as God setting His foreknowledge in stone. He stated that nobody can deviate and ultimately concluded that no one has free will.

Calvin, third and contrary to his no-deviation opinion, teaches that predestination means that those who were the best of the best in their videos are God's special elect people whom He predestined to deviate and perform special jobs for Him. They earned a special deviation permission slip.

Calvin said God foresaw His elect as worthy. However, he contradicts himself by saying that God intervenes in their life and gives them a new heart. He states that nobody can go to heaven without a special intervention and a special salvation experience.

If the elect's videos showed them entering heaven without intervention from God, why on earth — pardon the pun — would they now need interference in their real lives? Calvin was over-stretching his imagination, trying hard to connect the dots, but ended up with a big ol' bowl of applesauce.

Calvin's condemned people didn't receive a special deviation slip and cannot deviate from their predestined damnation. If Father set everyone's ultimate destiny in stone, it would be pointless for Him to send special prophets to perform special tasks. Father isn't a time-waster.

There is no reasonable explanation of why God sent prophets to the unsavable damned. Why would He predestine anyone to do anything other than just let their real-life versions unfold exactly as He saw in their videos?

Calvin squeezed, twisted, and tangled the word 'predestined' to mean many things so it would fit into his fast-forward video, predestination-only, and no-free-will theories. Now, we'll need to untangle his bowl of applesauce and put all the apples back together correctly.

Predestined: Being pre-selected, pre-chosen, and pre-judged as worthy. Foreordained before entering the womb for an important task or purpose.

Justified: To be marked for a legitimate reason, declared, or made righteous in the eyes of God. Judged as righteous, declared free of guilt, and typically based on proven past actions.

Reason for future prophecies: It shows that God has an overall Master Plan and is completely in control of heaven and earth. In the future, people will see past prophecies come true, and they will realize the Bible is the Word of God. Knowing that our Father is real will encourage people to turn their hearts to loving Him. It also shows us that people have a choice — also known as free will.

God's plan: To die a fleshly death to pay for His children's deserved death penalty — for anyone who believes in Him, follows His commandments, and loves Him. Ultimately, it's so Father can remove all children who are corrupt and unreformable, so that His obedient children can live in peace, joy, love, and happiness.

Satan's plan: To corrupt and deceive God's children into following and worshiping him. The more children he corrupts, the more he hurts our Father.

Reason for preaching: It is so people can hear about heaven and turn their hearts toward loving our Father. It shows that people have a choice — also known as free will.

I knew you before you were in the womb: This shows a personal relationship that Jeremiah doesn't remember, but God does. 'Before' means prior to. 'I knew you before' means I knew you previously.

Calvin doesn't realize that he depicted God as not being all-knowing right before watching the alleged videos. If we confronted Calvin about this, he would backpedal and claim God is all-knowing because of His ongoing ability to watch videos. We must ask Calvin: if God already knew which people would go to heaven and hell, then why did God predestine preachers to preach to people who have no free will?

Why would Jesus say that whosoever believes in Him, loves Him, and follows His commandments can have eternal life? Wouldn't it be a waste of time to send preachers if nobody could choose to love our Father?

If God foreordained Jeremiah based on his remarkable behavior, it suggests that Jeremiah's actual life was different. Now he's a prophet. However, he wasn't a prophet in his video. Not only did Jeremiah's real life change, but everyone else's around him also shifted. Jeremiah is now preaching to them, whereas he wasn't in their videos. Everything must be exact for Calvin to say everyone is living a replica of their video. We can't add an orange to applesauce without turning the whole batch into something completely different. We would then have to call it orplesauce. The entire apple cart is upset if just one tiny thing varies.

Calvin would need to retract his exact-replica, no-deviation teaching. However, he would probably just backtrack and change his stance, claiming that Jeremiah's video showed him as a prophet, while everyone else's video showed them being preached to. If Calvin backtracked and claimed Jeremiah's real life was a replica of his video, then why did God predestine him in his video? What did Jeremiah do to deserve this honorable position? God is fair, and Jeremiah would have earned this position. Why didn't we all get chosen to be prophets?

Would Calvin then claim it was in an entirely different fast-forward video that Jeremiah earned his position? How many videos do we need to rewind to understand why God predestined him? Calvin's theory is quickly unraveling.

It makes no sense to send prophets to people who have no free will. Why would Father send out ministers to those who cannot do anything to be saved, cannot change their behavior, and cannot deviate from their predetermined destiny? Chasing after all of Calvin's opinions and theories is like trying to eat applesauce with a fork — or bobbing for apples in an empty barrel.

~ Apple Pie in the Sky ~

The only reasonable explanation for God sending prophets, teachers, and preachers is to spread the message of the kingdom of heaven. Father hopes people will love Him and choose His path of love. He wouldn't waste His time sending prophets and preachers if they couldn't help people. Calvin believed that God's reason for sending prophets was so that when people reject the preaching, God can pour more fiery coals on their heads in hell.

Besides portraying a cruel Father, adding more burning coals contradicts Calvin's no-deviation teaching. First, listening to newly added prophets is a deviation. Second, rejecting their preaching is also a deviation. Third, piling more coals upon their heads is another major deviation.

"Moreover whom he did predestinate, them he also called: and whom he called, them he also justified: and whom he justified, them he also glorified" (Rom 8:30).

Father justified or judged Jeremiah as righteous based on a legitimate reason. He proved himself worthy. Traveling through life and making fleshly mistakes didn't harm him or change God's previous judgment of him. God intervened in his free will and used him to prophesy and teach others about heaven.

Calvin contradicts his no-deviation teaching by portraying that God's elect are not simply living a copy of their video. He claims that, at His chosen time, God will intervene in their lives with a transformative salvation experience. He will strike them with deep sorrow for their sins, soften their hardened hearts, and give them a new heart that loves Him and longs to live a holy life.

Wait! What? Why would God need to intervene to make them different if their video showed them being worthy of heaven? If they displayed exceptional behavior and lived a nearly perfect life, no special intervention would be necessary. They could simply live out their real lives as shown in the video, and Father would take them to heaven. Allowing it to happen naturally would be enough. Plus, a special intervention for one person causes everyone else around them to act differently from what their video showed.

It's possible that Jeremiah was an exceptionally good person, but what about Saul, also known as Paul? Paul was persecuting, arresting, and having Christians stoned to death! I wouldn't see Paul's actions as proof that he deserved to be one of God's special elect. The Bible says that God struck down Paul on the way to Damascus, intervened in his life, and called him into service. But why? What did Paul do to earn being one of God's chosen people? When did Paul prove himself worthy? He certainly didn't prove his worth during his real life.

Calvin should have realized that his video theory didn't make sense when he read that Paul was the head honcho in charge of the genocide and religious cleansing of Christians. Paul, born with a bite, was a go-getter. He ferociously hated

Christians. If God had not intervened, Paul would have killed them all.

Calvin's theory falls apart when we see Paul acting horrifically. He wasn't doing great works, living a more perfect life, or being more loving than Calvin's allegedly doomed people. Jesus had to strike Paul to his knees to stop him from being a monster. If God intervenes for one monstrous child, then it's only fair for Him to intervene in every monstrous child's life. Father is fair, and like any good parent, what is fair for one child is fair for all. If one child gets an apple, then we all get an apple.

Calvin would cover his tracks by claiming that God saw in Paul's video that he later, near the end of his life, felt remorse for his actions. His later remorse made him worthy of being one of God's elect. After God's intervention, did Paul live a different real-life version — the one we now read about in the Bible? Was his previous fast-forward video magically erased?

We would need to ask Calvin: if that was correct, why did God intervene earlier in Paul's life to make him act differently than in his video? Why did God send Paul to preach if no one truly had a choice? Calvin would have to provide a reasonable explanation.

One excellent explanation for why God had Paul preach is so everyone could hear about heaven and choose it, which shows that people have free will. Calvin would never agree with this sound reasoning, as it wouldn't fit into his predestination-only and no-free-will narrative.

Besides his "more fiery coals" view, Calvin explained that the purpose of preaching was so that, when God sends everyone to hell, they can't complain that He didn't give them every opportunity to choose good. For Calvin, it was simply an extra safety measure to prevent anyone from arguing with God about going to hell.

Calvin denies that God sent Paul out to teach people how to be saved. According to Calvin, Paul's preaching did nothing for the predestined damned people. God has already determined their fate. Heaven for them is just one big apple pie in the sky that they can never reach.

If Paul's preaching couldn't help the unsaved, why would God intervene in his life to make him preach to them? God could have simply let the videos play out, and the outcome would have been favorable to Paul. According to his video, he would have eventually chosen Father's path without special intervention.

God is fair and doesn't play favorites. When God foreordained Jeremiah and Paul, they must have previously proven themselves trustworthy. They needed to earn the honorable assignments that God gave them.

When we compare apples to apples, Paul didn't earn his elect status in a video or in his real life, so the only other option is that Paul literally earned his honorable position before entering his mother's womb.

~ An Apple Per Day ~

Calvin's predestination-only and no-free-will opinions show extreme contradiction to Jesus' teachings. This inconsistency has caused much confusion among many people, making it nearly impossible for most to understand Calvin's theology.

Calvin claims that we have no free will and therefore cannot choose to love our Father. However, Jesus commanded us to love the Lord our God with all our heart, soul, strength, and mind. Jesus also taught that anyone who believes in Him, loves Him, and keeps His commandments will have eternal life. Jesus taught that we do have free will. Despite this, Calvin completely dismissed Jesus' teachings. He added predestination only and removed free will from the Word of God.

Just like one rotten apple spoils the whole barrel, Calvin has left his followers feeling hopeless. They believe they can't do anything to be saved or reach heaven after they die. Calvin taught them that their fate is entirely predestined and unchangeable — whatever shall be, shall be.

His followers always wonder about their destiny. However, they never take steps to develop a relationship with Father.

They keep waiting for Father to strike them down with a new heart salvation experience, like He did to Paul. They never find spiritual peace because they refuse to embrace Father's promises.

Calvin taught his parishioners that God's promises are meant only for His chosen few. Unless they are struck down like Paul, they must remain in the waiting room. They cannot open the door to the Doctor's Office unless the Doctor spiritually stabs them in the heart and destroys their fleshly lusts.

They can only enter the Doctor's office if the Doctor comes out to the waiting room and stabs them. The Doctor then gives them a new heart, and they will then have pure, holy thoughts and love God. Calvin taught that this new heart operation will only happen to God's elect. Calvin said we can't open the door to the Doctor's office, even though the Bible says we can:

"Behold, I stand at the door, and knock: if any man hear my voice, and open the door, I will come in to him, and will sup with him, and he with me" (Rev 3:20).

"Look unto me, and be ye saved, all the ends of the earth: for I am God, and there is none else" (Is 45:22).

God isn't a liar. The Doctor stands at everyone's heart door. If we fall into the category of any person, we must take the first step to open the door and invite Him in. It doesn't say that the Doctor opens the door for us. We must take the action of opening the door to show the Doctor that we want healing.

The Doctor won't force healing on us. We must ask and give Him permission for His treatment, then He will proceed with His healing. He will show us His way and His truth once we desire a relationship with Him.

Calvin instructs his followers to pray constantly for salvation, but then they reject the healing because their stabbing isn't painful enough. To them, being saved is a severe stabbing of guilt and shame from which they don't recover. They beg the Doctor repeatedly, but never open the door to His office.

They believe that the Doctor's stabbing will cause them to feel extreme sorrow, grief, and endless crying. Periodically, they all feel remorse for their sins. However, if they feel better the next day, they conclude that the stabbing wasn't from God. It must be severe depression before they consider it real. As they keep eating Calvin's poisoned apples — one per day — they definitely keep the Doctor away!

Calvin portrayed Father as angry, cruel, judgmental, unmerciful, unloving, and distant. Father didn't need to create Earth or people. Our loving Father wouldn't have wasted His time creating billions of people just to cast most of them into eternal fire. Father wouldn't have made billions of rotten apples when He could have simply created only the good apples.

Father is loving, has perfect common sense, and holds ultimate power. If watching videos were His thing, He would have an endless supply. He would have picked a video that would have led to a much better outcome for everyone involved.

Calvin depicts God as extremely limited, having only this one video option. Although God has unlimited power and majestic abilities, He could have created everyone without free will and programmed them to love. He could have made only the loving people — if watching videos was His kind of thing.

Calvin taught that God will cast the condemned into hell, where they will scream in torment forever. However, in Ezekiel 28:18, Father has judged and sentenced Satan to ashes. Father will blot him out.

Satan, the head honcho of the little rotten apples, will become a fried apple, turned to ashes, and he will never exist again. Father will do the same to all the spoiled apples that don't fall far from Satan's tree. Calvin said that the people in heaven can look over and see Aunt Mary screaming in pain. That sounds like bushels of fun, doesn't it? That sounds like a peaceful, heavenly home, doesn't it? No apples for the teacher on that opinion.

Calvin portrays everyone as having free will in their videos, but claims no one has a choice in their real life. A replica implies everything must be exactly the same. Father will not condemn anyone to hell if they have no free will. Instead, Father will judge everyone based on the choices they made with their free will.

His doctrine wobbles as he contradicts himself. Calvin states that God's elect can't be saved by doing good works, but only through God's grace. He explains that God foresaw the elect choosing to love Him, so He saved them from hell with His grace. Now, Calvin claims they do not get saved because of their real-life actions, but solely because of God's grace. Try to take a bite out of that apple.

John Calvin's views on Judgment Day and hell are also confusing and contradictory. He said that when people die, their spirits — without bodies — immediately go to heaven or hell. He believed that when Jesus returns at His second coming, every soul will re-enter its decayed flesh body. Calvin states that God will restore all the dead bodies to perfect condition, and everyone will rise out of the graves to stand before God. He calls this the resurrection of the dead.

Calvin describes Judgment Day as a one-day reprieve for the souls in hell. He states they will return to their flesh bodies. After Father announces their judgment, He will send them back to hell — this time with their flesh bodies. Those in heaven also need to change bodies — first into their decayed flesh for Judgment, then into their spiritual bodies to reenter heaven.

Calvin teaches that only people's spirits go to heaven or hell when they die. Lazarus and the rich man both had bodies in heaven and hell. They could see and talk to each other across the gulf that separated them. The wealthy man wanted water to cool his tongue. To have a tongue, he would also have had a body. It wasn't his flesh body, as that was back on Earth in the graveyard.

"And it came to pass, that the beggar died, and was carried by the angels into Abraham's bosom: the rich man also died, and was buried; And in hell he lift up his eyes, being in torments, and seeth Abraham afar off, and Lazarus in his bosom. And he cried and said, Father Abraham, have mercy on me, and send Lazarus, that he may dip the tip of his finger in water, and cool my tongue; for I am tormented in this flame" (Lu 16:22-24).

Lazarus in Abraham's bosom — hugging Abraham — illustrates that they have bodies. Everyone who has died a fleshly death has entered their spiritual body. There is no need for anyone to body-hop on Judgment Day. The Bible says flesh and blood cannot enter the kingdom of heaven. The Throne of God is in heaven. Heaven is wherever God is. Only the spiritual body can enter the spiritual realm to receive judgment.

"Then shall the dust return to the earth as it was: and the spirit shall return unto God who gave it" (Ecc 12:7).

When we die, our spirit leaves the flesh and returns to God. Father put each of our spirits, and His own Spirit, into a flesh body. His name is Yeshua — Joshua in Hebrew — or Jesus in English. When Jesus died in the flesh, His Spirit re-entered His spiritual body.

The resurrection of the dead means that when we die, our spirit leaves our flesh bodies and enters into — or rises into — our spiritual bodies. This change of bodies happens at the exact moment of death. Calvin claimed that the resurrection of the dead means everyone will rise from their graves. He was mistaken. When Jesus returns, everyone transforms into spiritual bodies, as we will prove next:

"But some man will say, How are the dead raised up? and with what body do they come?" (1 Cor 15:35).

The question being asked is, "How do the dead enter into a spiritual body? What bodies will they have when they return with Jesus?

"Thou fool, that which thou sowest is not quickened, except it die. And that which thou sowest, thou sowest not that body that shall be, but bare grain, it may chance of wheat, or of some other grain. There are also celestial bodies and bodies terrestrial" (1 Cor 15:36-37, 40).

Our flesh body must die so our spirit can resurrect into our spiritual body. An apple tree grows after the apple seed dies in the ground. The celestial body is our heavenly body. The terrestrial body is the flesh body.

"So also is the resurrection of the dead. It is sown in corruption; it is raised in incorruption" (1 Cor 15:42).

The resurrection of the dead is the entering into the spiritual body. Sown in corruption means that the flesh body dies and is buried in the ground. Raised in incorruption refers to when our spirit is raised, resurrected, or enters our spiritual body.

"It is sown a natural body; it is raised a spiritual body" (1 Cor 15:44).

The natural body is the flesh. It is raised — or will enter into a spiritual body.

"And as we have borne the image of the earthy, we shall also bear the image of the heavenly" (1 Cor 15:49).

As we, our soul and spirit, entered the earthly flesh body, we shall also bear the heavenly — celestial — spiritual body.

"Now this I say, brethren, that flesh and blood cannot inherit the kingdom of God; neither doth corruption inherit incorruption" (1 Cor 15:50).

Corruption is our terrestrial, flesh body. Incorruptibility pertains to our celestial, or spiritual body. Flesh cannot enter heaven, nor can it enter our heavenly body.

"Behold, I shew you a mystery; We shall not all sleep, but we shall all be changed" (1 Cor 15:51).

A mystery? Sleep means to die a natural death. However, everyone will change into their celestial bodies.

"In a moment, in the twinkling of an eye, at the last trump: for the trumpet shall sound, and the dead shall be raised incorruptible, and we shall be changed" (1 Cor 15:52).

"In the twinkling of an eye" means instantaneously. Jesus returns at the seventh trump, which is the last trumpet. When the trumpet sounds, the dead, flesh, corruptible bodies will be raised, meaning we will enter into our incorruptible, celestial, spiritual bodies.

"For this corruptible must put on incorruption and this mortal must put on immortality" (1 Cor 15:53).

Our corruptible body must change into an incorruptible, celestial, spiritual body. Mortal means capable of dying. Immortality means being incapable of death.

"So when this corruptible shall have put on incorruption and this mortal shall have put on immortality, then shall be brought to pass the saying that is written, Death is swallowed up in victory" (1 Cor 15:54).

Our corruptible, flesh, terrestrial body will put on our incorruptible, celestial, spiritual body. Our mortal — able to die — body will put on our immortal — unable to die body.

The question in verse 35 was: when people die, how does their spirit get raised up? How does it enter into the spiritual body? What bodies will they have when they come back with Jesus?

Flesh and blood are terrestrial, corruptible, and mortal, so they cannot enter the spiritual realm. Our spiritual body is celestial, incorruptible, and immortal. It's what our spirit instantly is raised up into, resurrects into, and enters into when our flesh body dies.

People who have died have already resurrected into their spiritual bodies. Everyone returning with Jesus will be in spiritual bodies. The flesh dimension disappears instantly. "The dead shall be raised" means that those in flesh bodies when Jesus returns will instantly die and change into their celestial bodies. From that moment on, the spiritual dimension will be all that exists.

We do not need our flesh bodies again. Every soul immediately enters its spiritual body at the moment of death, whether that happens before Jesus' return or at the instant of His return. The spiritual body is the only body that can approach God's Judgment Seat. Flesh and blood cannot enter the kingdom of heaven — and heaven is wherever God is. No flesh bodies will be approaching God.

~ The Big Apple ~

Calvin's teaching about the death of infants concerns me. He stated that babies are born guilty of Adam and Eve's sin in the Garden of Eden. He claimed some babies go to heaven and others go to hell. Infant damnation conflicts with his fast-forward video theory, which teaches that each person's acceptance into heaven depends on their works that God foresaw them doing.

Babies don't have any works, but according to Calvin, they are all guilty. Calvin leaves his parishioners in unnecessary grief, always wondering if their baby went to heaven or hell. Then, contradictorily, he teaches that infants must be baptized, so he must have believed that baptizing babies gives them a better chance of going to heaven if they die.

Baptism does not grant access to heaven. The thief on the cross was never baptized. However, when Jesus saw that his heart was repentant, Jesus told him: "Today shalt thou be with me in paradise" (Lu 23:43).

The thief went to heaven, so babies, children, and adults can enter heaven without being baptized. Jesus knows our hearts, and that's what determines whether we enter heaven. Baptism is simply an act of obedience and not a qualification for heaven.

Calvin believed that nobody can enter heaven without baptism. He thought that if a baby died and God had predestined it to heaven, then it needed to be baptized as soon as possible after birth. He believed that all unbaptized babies went to hell.

"And Jesus, when he was baptized, went up straightway out of the water" (Mt 3:16).

Jesus was baptized as an adult. He didn't get sprinkled with water; John submerged Jesus in the water, so it would be proper to follow His example. Baptism is an act of obedience and a public declaration that we want to live for Jesus. Babies cannot understand what baptism is or what it signifies, nor can they choose to give their lives to Jesus, so baptizing babies makes no sense.

Baptizing by submerging and reemerging symbolizes the death and resurrection of Jesus. It represents the submerging of our old, sinful self and the reemergence as a new spiritual person with Jesus in us. It shows that we've chosen to circumcise our hearts, cutting off the old sinful nature, and are committing to live a life that pleases our Father.

"And John also was baptizing in Aenon near to Salim, because there was much water there: and they came, and were baptized" (Jn 3:23).

The large amount of water being used shows that John was baptizing people by immersion. If John only needed to sprinkle water on foreheads, he wouldn't have required an area with lots of water. Every house had a few extra sprinkles if that was all he needed.

Sprinkling or submerging babies in water does not determine whether a baby goes to heaven. Our loving Father won't hold babies and children accountable for their actions until they reach the age of accountability. That age varies depending on each person's life circumstances, traumas they've experienced, and their mental development.

We must actively choose to believe in Jesus, turn away from sin, and dedicate our lives to Him. Once we make that commitment, we can be baptized as a sign of our obedience and love for Him.

Parents can hold a baby dedication ceremony, anoint their child, and ask Father to protect them as we raise them in this tumultuous world.

Calvin taught that we must be baptized to enter heaven. His claim is incorrect because the thief did not get baptized. Calvin said nobody can choose to give their life to Jesus, so he rejected adult baptism, where a person decides for themself.

Calvin said we must be ‘born again' to go to heaven, which he interpreted as receiving a new heart or a special salvation experience from God. He's correct that to enter heaven, we have to circumcise our hearts and become a new person. However, he doesn't provide the proper definition of being born again. Being born again and being born of the Spirit are two different things.

"Jesus answered and said unto him, Verily, verily, I say unto thee, Except a man be born again, he cannot see the kingdom of God" (Jn 3:3).

Again - Strong's G509 from the original #507; born from above.

We cannot enter the kingdom of heaven unless we are 'born from above.'

"Jesus answered, Verily, verily, I say unto thee, Except a man be born of water and of the Spirit, he cannot enter into the kingdom of God" (Jn 3:5).

Jesus specified two requirements. Being born of water means being born from our mother's bag of waters in her womb. To be born of the Spirit means to invite Jesus into our hearts. We cannot enter heaven unless we meet both requirements.

"That which is born of the flesh is flesh; and that which is born of the Spirit is spirit" (Jn 3:6).

Calvin said that 'born of water' means a person must be baptized with water. We know this is incorrect because of the thief on the cross. Born of water refers to a flesh birth through our mother's amniotic fluid. Being born of the Spirit means inviting the Holy Spirit to dwell in us.

"And no man hath ascended up to heaven, but he that came down from heaven, even the Son of man which is in heaven" (Jn 3:13).

Coming down from above is equivalent to being born again — or born from above. Nobody can ascend to heaven unless they first descend from heaven, just as Jesus did. We must descend, come down from above, and be born into a flesh body through our mother's water bag.

Then, to ascend back into heaven, we must also be born of the Spirit. If we do not invite Father's Spirit to live in us, we may not enter our Father's wondrous and magical heaven. Why people aren't daily striving to join this fantastic place for eternal life with our loving Father is beyond my understanding. It's the most beautiful and best place. It's The Big Apple!

Being born of the Spirit means we believe Jesus came in the flesh and paid the price for our sins with His death. By repenting of our sins, we open the door of our hearts and invite Jesus in. Desiring a Poppa-child relationship, we live our lives for Him and resist the old, sinful self. Focusing on Him, we choose what pleases Him. To live life daily in harmony with His Spirit of peace and love inside us. Loving our Poppa is a choice.

We must be cleansed of our sins through Jesus' blood. He paid the death penalty for anyone who believes in Him, loves Him, and follows His commandments. We walk a path not driven by our old fleshly lusts and desires, but by what God desires for us. Our goal is to please Him and to strive for perfection in love toward Him and others.

Satan and his evil angels have refused to enter a flesh body, so they can never go to heaven. They all knew the rules before they broke them. No spirit may descend to earth without being born of water through the womb. When a spirit comes to earth illegally, they automatically relinquish their entrance to heaven.

Satan forfeited heaven when he illegally came to the Garden of Eden to deceive Adam and Eve. Since he was not born into a flesh body, he cannot enter heaven. Before Noah's flood, angels came to Earth without being born of a woman, so they also forfeited their rights to enter heaven.

Calvin's teaching of the Trinity — that one God is three persons — is also confusing. He said there's only one God, but that God reveals Himself as three distinct persons who carry out three different tasks. The church I grew up in described the Trinity as the Father sitting on His throne, the Son being a fleshly person, and the Spirit as a ghost-like figure we can't see. It was never explained to me how these three separate entities could be just one God.

Calvin never taught that God's Spirit inhabits a body just as our spirit and consciousness inhabit our body. God is much more than His body. All energy belongs to Him and is Him. He has consciousness, intellect, thoughts, and feelings. Although Father has many names, one of His names is Jesus. His flesh name is Jesus. Our spiritual body's name is the same as our flesh body's name. Our name has nothing to do with which body our mind and personality dwell in.

Father has infinite energy and consciousness that extends out forever. He wanted to interact with His children without being the size of the universe, which would likely terrify us. So, Father — Jesus — has the same body size as we do, so He can interact with us without frightening us with His enormous energy.

Father might also have another spiritual body sitting on a massive throne somewhere. I'm definitely not going to tell Father how many bodies He can have, how big they are, or what size throne He can sit on. He told Moses that His name is: "I am that I am," which means: "I am whatever I choose to be," so I interpret that as He will be whatever form He chooses, whenever He chooses. He can have as many bodies as He pleases, if He decides to have more than one.

Father showed Himself to Moses as a burning bush. I can barely wrap my head around it, and I'll be the last person to limit Father, who has no limits. Anyone can count the number of seeds in an apple, but only God can count the number of apples in a seed.

Father's body is all energy that exists. His Spirit is His consciousness and intellect. Father, also known as Jesus, put His Spirit into a flesh body that is in the image of His spiritual body. Our spirits also entered into flesh bodies. We will all be together soon, and what our puny little minds can't understand now, we will know the moment Jesus returns.

Our soul is who we are — our personality — our heart, compassion, and feelings. Our spirit is our intellect, our ability to think, speak, learn, analyze, and choose. The physical form is the body that our spirit and soul inhabit. We have two bodies: one celestial and one terrestrial. One is spiritual; the other is flesh. Evil spirits can take up residence in our mental housing and manipulate our thinking negatively. God's Spirit can also dwell in us and guide our thoughts positively. Evil spirits enter people without invitation. The only way to prevent evil spirits from inhabiting our minds is to invite our Father — Jesus — into our hearts as our Protector.

As we peel back the layers, Calvin's theology is confusing, contains misinterpretations and incorrect definitions, is vague, and completely falls apart upon close examination. Its complexity explains why his followers don't ask questions about the details of his predestination-only theory. They don't see Calvin's opinions as ideas or theories. Instead, they see his doctrine as the Big Apple, the biggest, the best, and as God's absolute truth.

Calvin's followers don't question God, and by extension, they don't question Calvinism. They say God's reasons are beyond our understanding. They believe that God hides knowledge and understanding from us, and if we can't understand something, then God doesn't want us to understand it. So, they just continue down their path of never fully understanding or seeking a logical answer. They never look for an answer that shows God to be fair and loving. Instead, they think God is a time-waster who sent preachers just to heap more fiery coals on the heads of most of His children.

Calvin spread this lie to their ancestors hundreds of years ago when he couldn't understand or explain his own teachings. Passed down through the generations, many people believe his lie today. They don't find it strange that they believe in and would die for a religion they don't fully comprehend and can't explain to others.

It's common for them to dismiss things they can't understand or explain. They use Calvin's same easy-out phrases, such as, *That's God's business. *God's thoughts are higher than our thoughts. *We're not meant to understand. *We're not to question why God does anything. Calvin relied on these easy-out phrases to avoid answering tough, in-depth questions about his theology.

"For God is not the author of confusion, but of peace, as in all churches of the saints" (1 Cor 14:33).

God does not create confusing doctrines that don't bring us peace. Father wants us to understand. If we pray for wisdom and understanding, He will give it to us.

Calvin projected an attitude of religious superiority toward outsiders — those of us who can't understand his confusing, twisted opinions. Calvin suggested that only special, intelligent individuals can comprehend his doctrine. He implied that if we don't believe his teachings, then we haven't received this special truth from God.

His followers say things like: *If God didn't make you believe Calvin, then you're one of the condemned. *The predestined damned will never understand John Calvin's truth. *Whoever believes Calvin's doctrine has a better chance of entering heaven.

To them, John Calvin was God's chosen holy man who delivered God's only truth. They don't realize they are following a man and his opinions. If it makes our head spin, fries our brain, or is so confusing that we can't wrap our head around it, if it feels like trying to force a square peg into a round hole, then it's best to keep looking for something that doesn't make us so dizzy.

There's no point in debating with Calvin's followers because they don't rely on scripture. Instead, they debate you with Calvin's unprovable, fast-forward video opinions. They don't compare apples to apples. They twist scripture to fit Calvin's theories because they genuinely believe that God watching fast-forward videos is true and scriptural. God told

Jeremiah, "Before you were in the belly, I knew you." Father did not say, "I knew of you," and He didn't say, "I watched a fast-forward video of you."

If you try to prove John Calvin wrong, his followers will see you as a lost sinner destined for hell. They will shake the dust off their feet, branding you as a heretic who refuses to listen. Becoming sour like a green apple, they will give you the cold shoulder as if you carry a highly contagious free-will disease. Then, they will mock you behind your back.

Calvin's followers will deem you a crazy free-willer who doesn't have God's exclusive truth. They cannot fully explain or prove Calvin's fast-forward video and no-free-will opinions from scripture, so they continually resort to saying that not everyone can understand. They consider themselves God's chosen people, the only wise apples that can understand Calvin's ideas.

You could accept Calvin's confusing and contradictory opinion that everyone earns heaven or hell based on God watching fast-forward videos — you do you — but since predestination-only was Calvin's baby, and no-free-will was his bathwater, I am going to throw the baby out with the bathwater.

Suppose Calvin's theories make your head spin, fry your brain, and confuse you to the point where you want to throw it all out the window. In that case, the only other option we have is that God predestined certain people to do special tasks for Him — based on their actual past actions before they entered their mother's womb.

Jesus said that whosoever believes in Him shall have eternal life, which shows that we have free will. Predestination has nothing to do with videos showing a preview of Judgment Day. Since Calvin's fast-forward videos, set-in-stone, no-deviation, and no-free-will opinions are the opposite of what Jesus taught, I reject Calvin's definitions of predestination.

For one to believe in predestination only, they have to reject free will entirely. If we accept that God created people with free will, then we admit that God doesn't know everyone's future choices. He doesn't know who will choose to love Him. He desires all to do so, which is why He sent prophets, preachers, and teachers.

If we believe in both predestination and free will, we must ask how this can be? And why did our Father predestine some people but not others for special tasks? What did these predestined people do to earn being chosen to assist our Father? When exactly did they prove themselves trustworthy and earn such honorable positions?

~ Apples and Worms ~

John Calvin could only fathom his video idea as how God knew Jeremiah before he entered his mother's womb. He believed it was the only fair way for God to predestine certain people for special tasks.

Calvin willfully ignored the possibility that God's predestination could literally be based on our having an actual prior existence, actual works, and actual trust built before our spirit entered our flesh body. Since Calvin neglected to play out this possibility, to be fair, we have to take a second bite of the apple to get down to the core and expound on this other plausible option as well.

There are literally only two options to explain why God told Jeremiah, "I knew thee" before you entered your mother's womb: 1) Calvin's fast-forward video idea, or 2) An actual and literal existence and prior relationship with our Father.

A long time ago, Father created the earth. Afterwards, He created His little angel children and placed them into spiritual bodies. He inserted a tiny spirit of consciousness into them so they could speak, learn, think, observe, create, and feel. He put His children on His newly formed earth and provided everything they needed to survive.

Our spirits inhabit bodies. Currently, our spirits occupy flesh bodies. When this flesh body dies, our spirit moves on to a celestial and immortal body.

Using their free will, some children became rebellious and disobedient. They are called evil or unclean spirits. If someone is angry, mean, and hateful, they might be an evil, unclean spirit. Otherwise, an evil spirit might be influencing their thoughts, words, and actions. The Bible offers insight into how this all works:

> For he said unto him, Come out of the man, thou unclean spirit. And he asked him, What is thy name? And he answered, saying, My name is Legion: for we are many. And all the devils besought him, saying, Send us into the swine, that we may enter into them. And forthwith Jesus gave them leave. And the unclean spirits went out, and entered into the swine: and the herd ran violently down a steep place into the sea, (they were about two thousand;) and were choked in the sea. (Mk 5:8-9, 12-13)

The herd of pigs drowned in the sea. The unclean spirits did not drown. They had to leave the dead pigs and search for another living host body to inhabit. Jesus could have commanded them to go back to hell and never return. However, He allowed them to remain on Earth for our target practice. He gave us power over all our enemies — including all evil spirits — and Satan himself.

"Behold, I give unto you power to tread on serpents and scorpions, and over all the power of the enemy: and nothing shall by any means hurt you" (Lu 10:19).

In Jesus' name, we can command Satan and all evil spirits to leave. We must cast out evil spirits in Jesus' name because we do not have the power to do it. Jesus is the source of all power.

We only have power over our enemies if Jesus' Spirit is within us. It is Jesus who handles the waste removal. To gain Father's protection, we must invite His Spirit into our minds, asking Him to stay with us and keep us safe.

We see that 2000 unclean, evil spirits can enter one person. They can also enter pigs. Our spirits will enter a celestial body when they leave this flesh body. Before our spirits entered our flesh, we previously inhabited a spiritual body.

Our spirit is the intellect and mind of our soul. Our soul is our self, our consciousness, heart, feelings, compassion, or personality. For example, when we hear someone say, "He doesn't have a soul," they mean, "He has no heart," or "He lacks compassion," or "His soul is rotten." A person with a hardened soul won't help a wounded man lying on the street.

Our celestial body lives in the spiritual realm. Our flesh body is to navigate the flesh realm. Both realms are different dimensions. No matter which body we inhabit, our soul and spirit live inside each.

Our spirit-soul can body-hop into different bodies. Our spirit-soul hopped into a flesh body when we entered our mother's belly in this flesh dimension. When the flesh dies, everyone's spirit-soul will enter their spiritual body in the spiritual dimension.

There are many good little spirits. Father has a Spirit that is perfect and holy. He is the main Holy Spirit who created us, and we will always return to Him. Good spirits desire the Holy Spirit's wisdom inside them, to lead and guide them in all things that are good and pleasing to Him.

The bad little spirits are hateful, evil, deceiving, and harmful people. If someone premeditates murder, they have an evil spirit inside them. We sometimes call these people little devils. Satan is our Father's enemy, and he possesses a deceiving and seducing spirit. He is the main evil spirit leading many of Father's children to do bad things. He is the big devil, or the primary evil spirit.

All spirits can body hop and penetrate people's minds. We must have the Holy Spirit within us as our protection against evil spirits who might manipulate our thoughts, feelings, actions, or words.

Father predestined Paul to be a preacher and a writer. Paul preached to thousands of people and wrote most of the New Testament. Father knew He could trust Paul to do this work for Him. Paul had proven himself trustworthy before his spirit entered his flesh body.

"For this they willingly are ignorant of, that by the word of God the heavens were of old, and the earth standing out of the water and in the water: whereby the world that then was, being overflowed with water, perished: but the heavens and the earth, which are now, by the same word are kept in store, reserved unto fire against the day of judgment and perdition of ungodly men" (2 Pet 3:5-7).

People are willingly ignorant that the heavens were of old, and the earth was standing in and out of the water. It looked similar to how Earth looks today. Many theologians say this refers to Noah's flood. However, nobody willfully ignores or is willingly ignorant of Noah's flood. Still, many people willingly keep themselves ignorant because they refuse to consider that we literally existed in a previous heaven and earth age.

Perished - Strong's G622 - To destroy fully.

"The world that then was, being overflowed with water, perished," meaning it became utterly destroyed.

Calvin said this refers to Noah's flood. Once again, Calvin proves himself unable to interpret word definitions correctly. The word 'perished' means that the world in question was completely and utterly destroyed. No birds and no humans remained. Nothing survived at all — end of story.

Noah's flood did not demolish the earth. We still have all the animals and people from different ethnic backgrounds. A dove flew out of the ark, and when it found a living olive tree, it brought back a leaf to Noah. God doesn't make mistakes. If Father used the word "perished" and that word means 'fully destroyed,' then we are not talking about Noah's flood.

The heavens and the earth, which are now, show that this is a different heaven and earth age than the one that God destroyed by overflowing it with water. It's the same Earth, as evidenced by the dinosaur fossils found on every continent. However, it is a different age, with different bodies and no dinosaurs. Dinosaurs would have been quite disastrous for flesh-and-blood people.

"Whose voice then shook the earth: but now he hath promised, saying, Yet once more I shake not the earth only, but also heaven" (Heb 12:26).

Father rattled the earth once before, and He will shake it again. He will eliminate all evil. Only the good will remain.

"Where wast thou when I laid the foundations of the earth? … When the morning stars sang together, and all the sons of God shouted for joy? (Job 38:4, 7).

Father is talking about a different laying of the foundations than when He created Adam and Eve. All of His beautiful little angel children used to be happy — singing and shouting for joy. It was an earlier time, during the age of dinosaurs.

"Behold now behemoth, which I made with thee … He moveth his tail like a cedar … Behold, he drinketh up a river, and hasteth not: he trusteth that he can draw up Jordan into his mouth" (Job 40:15, 17, 23).

Only dinosaurs have tails the size of a cedar tree. Only dinosaurs think they can drink enormous amounts of water. It believes it can drink the entire Jordan River. It says God created the behemoth — the dinosaur — with Job. Since Father created Job in the dinosaur age, I would bet my boots that He created us at that same time as well!

Before we entered the flesh age, we existed during the age of the dinosaurs — the first Earth age. This age was when Satan, with his free will, rebelled against God. Satan had earned the position of top lieutenant. He was a cherub that covered the Mercy Seat of Jesus. Over time, his beauty, riches, and position went to his head. Pride, arrogance, jealousy, and iniquity entered his heart, turning him rotten to the core. Instead of guarding and protecting Jesus' seat, Satan wanted to sit on it.

Satan let his ego flare and wanted everyone to admire him. He deceived many of the sons of God — the stars of heaven — the little angel children, into giving him praise, honor, and worship instead of our Father. Satan was a good apple that went rotten.

"Thou hast been in Eden the garden of God … Thou art the anointed cherub that covereth … Thou wast perfect in thy ways from the day that thou wast created, till iniquity was found in thee" (Ez 28:13-15).

Satan used to be a perfect little angel child. Father loved him very much. Satan loved Father very much as well. He had earned a prominent position and was the apple of our Father's eye. Then, as a worm enters an apple, pride, arrogance, jealousy, iniquity, and rebellion entered Satan's egotistical heart, and he turned very rotten.

Jeremiah and Paul didn't fall for Satan's deception. They were powerful leaders who stood strong for our Father during Satan's rebellion. Because of that, they were justified. They earned the right to be Father's elect to perform special tasks during this flesh, second earth age.

Father was furious with Satan for deceiving one-third of His children. He was angry with His rebellious children, who followed Satan and worshipped him. The punishment for their rebellion was death. It may have crossed Father's mind just to get rid of all the rotten apples. He could have blotted them all out. However, He loves them all very much. Disposing of children you love is almost impossible.

Parents always hope that the worm will crawl out of the rotten apple. They hope their child will someday begin making good choices, apologize, and become a good little apple again.

Choosing not to destroy His rebellious children, Father instead performed a great reset and wiped out that first earth age — the era when we sang and shouted for joy — the age of the dinosaurs. It's from that age that archaeologists found a perfectly preserved mammoth with buttercups still in its mouth and stomach in the tundra of Alaska.

Father wants His children to return to loving Him. However, even if they come back to Him, they still have to pay their penalty of death for their rebellion and worship of Satan.

Father decided to pay the death penalty for everyone who would apologize and love Him again. That's exactly what all good Poppas would do for their children. The only way Poppa could pay the death price was to enter a flesh body.

Father's spiritual body can never die. His second Earth Age plan provides everyone — including Himself — the ability to enter flesh bodies. Those who refuse, such as Satan and his minions, won't be able to claim Jesus' flesh death as their payment for the price they owe.

Calvin couldn't comprehend that Father had created us alongside the dinosaurs and that we were all alive when Satan rebelled against Father. Calvin knew God was fair, and he believed that predestination was based on fairness. Still, he simply couldn't grasp that everyone physically existed and had literal actions during a previous age. If the idea even crossed Calvin's mind, he wasn't brave enough to entertain it. Calvin probably would have been burned at the stake for heresy or maybe forced to bob for apples if he had even dared to explore it further.

Father could have created us without free will and forced us to love Him. However, He knows that forced love is fake love. Father's desire was for us to choose to love Him — because we appreciate and respect Him. We all desire genuine love from others, and nobody enjoys receiving insincere or forced love. Our Father feels the same way. He wanted us to desire a Poppa-child relationship out of our own free will.

Everyone loved Father. However, because of free will — just like an apple will always roll downhill — and just like the worm will find a way into the apple, Satan became the sour apple that turned the entire apple cart upside down.

All people still have free will in the Second Age. Father still desires genuine love from us. God's elect did not follow or worship Satan. They have proven themselves to be top-notch, and Father judged them as righteous. Father can intervene in their flesh lives to use them as He needs in His effort to recoup some of His little angel children.

"And no man hath ascended up to heaven, but he that came down from heaven, even the Son of man which is in heaven" (Jn 3:13).

We can't ascend to heaven unless we first come down from there. Even Jesus descended first and then ascended back into heaven after His flesh death.

"Forasmuch then as the children are partakers of flesh and blood, he also himself likewise took part of the same; that through death he might destroy him that had the power of death, that is, the devil" (Heb 2:14).

We all partake of a flesh body. Our little angel spirit entered the flesh, and likewise, our Father did the same.

"Except a man be born again, he cannot see the kingdom of God" (Jn 3:3).

Born again - Strong's G507 - born from above.

Born again means to come from above. We can't enter heaven unless we first descend from above. Our spirits must enter a flesh body.

"This is he that came by water and blood, even Jesus Christ; not by water only, but by water and blood" (1 Jn 5:6).

The main reason we are here in this fleshly existence is so Father could die to pay the penalty for those who earned death. This flesh age is His beautiful plan to give the rebellious children the opportunity to return to Him, so they can once again sing and shout for joy.

"And God said, Let us make man in our image, after our likeness" (Gen 1:26).

Let us — God and the angels — make flesh people a replica of us. Using the words "us" and "our" shows that God was speaking to His little angels who were surrounding Him. Father had a spiritual body in the first age. His name was Jesus then as well. Father created flesh bodies to mirror their spiritual bodies. Let's make our flesh bodies look just like we look now.

After our flesh body dies, we will re-enter our celestial body. I'm not an expert on spiritual bodies, but our previous body might still be inside us. When we die, we will leave our flesh and return to the heavenly realm. Father may have a new spiritual body for us to enter when we return to Him. The Bible doesn't go into detail. Still, I can't imagine that our previous spiritual body is just hanging on a coat rack somewhere, waiting for our spirit to enter it. But who knows — all things are possible with God.

~ Rotten to the Core ~

Many people find it hard to believe that we once coexisted with the dinosaurs. It's beyond their imagination that we lived when Satan grew prideful and took his ego on a trip down primrose lane. Many people will want to scream into a pillow for about an hour, thinking it's blasphemous to suggest such a thing.

Father suppressed our memories of what happened so that everyone could make choices without being influenced by our past. He didn't want memories affecting our current decisions about whom to love and serve. He gave everyone a clean mental slate and didn't want us remembering if we had rebelled or were deceived by Satan — possibly even worshiping him with all his musical instruments and pipes. Today, many people are on the same slippery slope — worshiping music stars and television celebrities.

Looking beyond the veil that covers our fleshly eyes, we can imagine Satan — filled with pride — desiring to sit on the Mercy Seat and wanting to be worshiped. He traveled from city to city, hosting concerts with his minions as his cast, musical staff, and drummers. Just like today, Satan used the same rotten, filthy, vulgar music to corrupt and promote his agenda. He tricked many people into worshiping him instead of our Father.

"The workmanship of thy tabrets and of thy pipes was prepared in thee in the day that thou wast created" (Ez 28:13).

Satan was quite the rock star with all of his tabrets and pipes.

"And there appeared another wonder in heaven; and behold a great red dragon, having seven heads and ten horns, and seven crowns upon his heads" (Rev 12:3).

This verse is talking about the First Earth Age. Satan — the dragon — and his evil angels had built a massive one-world system under their control. The seven heads represent seven nations, the ten horns stand for ten power systems, and the seven crowns symbolize seven kings or leaders who ruled over the seven nations.

It's no different today in this second age. Satan still uses the same tactics, and his ultimate goal is still to dominate a one-world system where everyone is under his control and worships him. Some of us will once again stand firm against him and stay loyal to our Heavenly Father.

"And his tail drew the third part of the stars of heaven, and did cast them to the earth" (Rev 12:4).

Satan deceived one-third of Father's angel children into following him and worshiping him. Through his great deception, Satan made the flesh age necessary so that Father, being a patient and loving Poppa, could pay the death penalty price for the deceived children. He hopes to recover some of His children by giving them the full opportunity to repent and return to loving Him.

Satan is the reason we all have to go through this flesh. If Satan hadn't done what he did, we would all still be in our spiritual bodies, singing and shouting for joy. If I were Father, I'd be angry too. Satan, in his arrogant pride and jealousy, made an enormous mess out of something so perfect.

Poppa doesn't want to destroy any of His children. He wants them to return to Him, love Him, and worship Him. Father's ultimate plan is to dispose of all the unreformable, irredeemable, and unrepentant children who are corrupt to the core, who love being rotten, and hence, will always be rotten to the core. They are a chip off the ol' rotten apple that they worship and call their father.

Those who return to loving Father with sincere repentance won't be liable to pay their death penalty. Poppa paid that price for them. We can't have a blissful and peaceful heaven with people who don't love Poppa. Those who refuse to love Him will have to pay the death penalty. Father will turn their spirit and soul to ashes. He will blot them out. You can bet yer boots that their little bubble of energy is on borrowed time.

The people whom Satan didn't deceive can still sometimes act like a rotten apple in this second age, as we saw with Paul. Satan is deceiving and corrupting as many people as possible and is taking full advantage of their temporary memory loss. They didn't worship Satan in the previous age, so their core isn't rotten. After they regain their memories, they will choose to love our Poppa.

Father used Jeremiah, Paul, and everyone that He has needed to make His flesh age plan come to complete fulfillment. He has done and will do whatever it takes to give those deceived by Satan a full opportunity to return to loving Him.

The people passionate about Father tried to warn the angel children not to follow Satan. They were remarkable leaders who loved Poppa with every cell in their spiritual bodies, and they stood strong against Satan and his deception. These incredible leaders worked hard to pull others away from chasing after Satan.

Because of their unwavering love for Father and their efforts to help His children, Jeremiah and Paul received appointments to carry out specific tasks in this second flesh age to continue striving to bring those rebellious children back to our Father.

Father decided not to destroy His rebellious children, but as we see next, He destroyed that earth age instead:

"I beheld the earth, and, lo, it was without form, and void; and the heavens, and they had no light" (Jer 4:23).

Without form - Strong's H8414 - to lie waste; a desolation, a worthless thing, in vain, confusion, empty place, without form, nothing, thing of nought, vain, vanity, waste, wilderness.

Earth was an empty wasteland wilderness.

Void - Strong's H922 - to be empty; a vacuity, an undistinguishable ruin, emptiness.

The earth was a vacuum, completely uninhabited, and an indistinguishable ruined wasteland wilderness, with no humans and no birds.

"I beheld the mountains, and, lo, they trembled, and all the hills moved lightly" (Jer 4:24).

Father, in His anger, did some massive shaking of the earth.

"I beheld, and, lo, there was no man, and all the birds of the heavens were fled" (Jer 4:25).

"I beheld, and, lo, the fruitful place was a wilderness, and all the cities thereof were broken down at the presence of the Lord, and by his fierce anger" (Jer 4:26).

Earth was a beautiful and fruitful place that once had cities, people, and birds. However, God, in His furious anger, shook it, overflowed it with water, and smashed it into an empty, indistinguishably ruined wasteland wilderness, which now has no people and no birds at all.

"For thus hath the Lord said, The whole land shall be desolate; yet will I not make a full end" (Jer 4:27).

Father could have ended it right then. He destroyed everything, but He chose not to dispose of all His rebellious angel children. He didn't throw out the little angel babies with the bathwater. The penalty for rebelling and worshiping anyone other than our Father is death.

Satan's ability to rebel against God shows us we were all created with free will. If Satan had free will, then everyone did. Those who did not fall for Satan's deception, those who remained steadfast for our Heavenly Father, were justified as righteous. They do not need to prove their trustworthiness again in this flesh age.

After the earth sat empty for an unspecified amount of time, Father established the second earth age — without dinosaurs.

"In the beginning God created the heaven and the earth" (Gen 1:1).

At this time, He also created the dinosaurs and Job. The first Earth age occurred between verses one and two.

"And the earth was without form, and void" (Gen 1:2).

Father, in His fierce anger, destroyed the first earth age. Father doesn't create things that are destroyed. It became that way because He demolished it in His furious anger. When Father creates, He creates perfection. He did not create the earth in shambles or as an empty, ruined, desolate, destroyed, wasteland wilderness mess. Some scholars say that the Hebrew translation from the manuscripts should read, "And the earth became without form and void."

Without Form - Strong's H8414 - to lie waste, a desolation of surface, a worthless thing, in vain, confusion, empty place, without form, nothing, thing of nought, vain, vanity, waste, wilderness.

Void - Strong's H922 - to be empty, a vacuity, an undistinguishable ruin, emptiness.

Earth was a horrific mess. Father didn't initially make it that way, as we see next:

"For thus saith the Lord that created the heavens; God himself that formed the earth and made it; he hath established it, he created it not in vain, he formed it to be inhabited: I am the Lord; and there is none else" (Is 45:18).

Vain - Strong's H8414 - to lie waste, a desolation, a worthless thing, in vain, confusion, empty place, without form, nothing, a thing of nought, vain, vanity, waste, wilderness, formlessness, confusion, unreality, emptiness, nothingness, empty space, that which is empty or unreal, place of chaos.

God did not create the earth in vain — without form — and void. He did not create it as an empty, indistinguishably ruined, destroyed, desolate, jumbled mess of a wasteland wilderness that had no man and no birds. He didn't create it without form and in a state of chaos. There would be no reason for our Father to create a destroyed, ice-covered earth for habitation and then later fine-tune it. That would be ridiculous, a waste of time, and pointless.

Father is a brilliant genius who creates everything perfect and beautiful. He never creates anything that is destroyed or in a chaotic mess. He said that when He formed Earth, He made it for habitation. Our Father isn't a time-waster.

Father, in His fierce anger, took out His massive wrecking ball, shook the earth, demolished it, tore down all the cities, overflowed it with water, and left nothing alive. Satan made Father furious. It was a real catastrophe. Father became outraged, and with the shizzy hittin' the fizzy, He destroyed that earth age — end of phase one.

We are now in phase two — the flesh age. It's not much different today. The only difference is that Satan isn't physically present among us. Still, his spirit and his angels' spirits are working overtime to deceive and corrupt as many of us as they can.

Our Heavenly Father is perfect, has no sin, and is pure and holy. He is everything and owns everything. He's so patient, loving, and kind that even if just one rebellious child returns to loving Him, it was worth His coming into flesh and being brutally murdered, even for that one child. Even if none of those rotten apples ever turn back to Him, His willingness to die and pay the penalty for those deserving death shows His deep love for all of us. He loves all of us very much!

So now, whether we choose to believe John Calvin's fast-forward video theory or that we all literally existed during the dinosaur age when Satan rebelled against our Father, at least we now have a couple of well-explained options to choose from. We can pick the one that makes the most sense to us. Either way, Poppa loves us all very much, and all He wants is that we choose to love Him too.

~ The Apple Tree ~

Father, in His fierce anger, destroyed the earth, shook it, and covered it with water. Then — when He was good and ready — after an unspecified amount of time, He began rebuilding the earth. Now, all of His angel children will enter a flesh body.

"And darkness was upon the face of the deep. And the Spirit of God moved upon the face of the waters" (Gen 1:2).

God is light. Our Father had abandoned the earth and removed His Spirit's light from it. He was furious and disgusted. Here, we see that water was already on the earth before God created anything. God didn't create the water on Day one. Father submerged the earth in an ice age of sorts.

"And God said, Let there be light: and there was light" (Gen 1:3).

"And God saw the light, that it was good: and God divided the light from the darkness. And God called the light Day, and the darkness he called Night. And the evening and the morning were the first day" (Gen 1:4-5).

This light is not the sun, as we'll soon see. Father creates the sun, moon, and stars on Day four. On Day One, God brought His Spirit to be a light upon the earth once again.

"And God said, Let there be a firmament in the midst of the waters, and let it divide the waters from the waters" (Gen 1:6).

Water covered the entire Earth. God placed a firmament — the sky — to separate the waters.

"And God made the firmament, and divided the waters which were under the firmament from the waters which were above the firmament: and it was so" (Gen 1:7).

God moved a massive amount of water off the earth, and He placed air — a firmament — between the two waters. As we will see in verse nine, water is still completely covering the earth at this point.

"And God called the firmament Heaven. And the evening and the morning were the second day" (Gen 1:8).

On Day Two, God made an enormous space of air. Wherever the air ends in space, there is a massive amount of water above it. That is why the sky looks blue.

"And God said, Let the waters under the heaven be gathered together unto one place, and let the dry land appear: and it was so" (Gen 1:9).

God withdrew all the water that covered the entire earth and shaped the oceans, seas, lakes, and rivers. Father did not create water during this rejuvenation process. He created water at the beginning of the dinosaur age, a long, long time ago.

"And God called the dry land earth; and the gathering together of the waters called he Seas: and God saw that it was good. And God said, Let the earth bring forth grass, the herb yielding seed, and the fruit tree yielding fruit after his kind, whose seed is in itself, upon the earth: and it was so" (Gen 1:10-11).

"And the earth brought forth grass, and herb yielding seed after his kind, and the tree yielding fruit, whose seed was in itself, after his kind: and God saw that it was good. And the evening and the morning were the third day" (Gen 1:12-13).

So, on Day Three, God pulled back the waters, forming the oceans, seas, lakes, and rivers. He also created the grass, trees, and plants.

"And God made two great lights; the greater light to rule the day, and the lesser light to rule the night: he made the stars also. And the evening and the morning were the fourth day" (Gen 1:16, 19).

On Day Four, God created the sun, the moon, and the stars.

"And God said, Let the waters bring forth abundantly the moving creature that hath life, and fowl that may fly above the earth in the open firmament of heaven. And the evening and the morning were the fifth day" (Gen 1:20, 23).

On Day Five, God created all the flying and water creatures.

"And God said, Let the earth bring forth the living creature after his kind, cattle, and creeping thing, and beast of the earth after his kind: and it was so" (Gen 1:24).

On Day Six, God created all the earth's animals and creeping things.

"And God said, Let us make man in our image, after our likeness ... So God created man in his own image, in the image of God created he him; male and female created he them" (Gen 1:26-27).

This is still Day Six. Father created all ethnicities of people. He made males and females at the same time on His sixth day of creation. Afterward, He placed all the various groups of people in different parts of the earth.

John Calvin doesn't teach that our Father created all ethnicities on the sixth day. He never explained how all the different people came to exist on Earth. We cannot say that all ethnicities originated from parents with the same skin color.

Calvin believed that different ethnicities on Earth resulted from a curse from God. I've never read in the Bible where God cursed someone and changed their skin color. It was just more of Calvin pulling weird things out of the ashes and sticking them where they don't belong. Calvin was so biblically illiterate that it's almost embarrassing.

Let us create man in our own image. Father was talking to His little angel children. We are all in the image of how we looked in the first Earth age.

"And God blessed them, and God said unto them, Be fruitful, and multiply, and replenish the earth" (Gen 1:28).

Replenish means to fill again and restore to a former level or condition. God doesn't make mistakes, so if He said to fill it again, that means Father had previously filled the earth with people.

John Calvin taught that when God said to 'replenish' the earth, He only meant to plenish it. Suppose Calvin was unable or unwilling to pick up a good ol' Webster's Dictionary to find that the word replenish means to fill again. In that case, he probably should have left interpreting the Bible to someone more qualified, someone who would know the definition of such a basic word.

"And God saw every thing that he had made, and, behold, it was very good. And the evening and the morning were the sixth day" (Gen 1:31).

The Bible doesn't specify the number of each ethnicity that God created.

"But, beloved, be not ignorant of this one thing, that one day is with the Lord as a thousand years, and a thousand years as one day" (2 Pet 3:8).

We don't know if each of these creation days was a literal 24-hour period or if each day represented 1000 years. We know the Day of the Lord — the millennium — lasts 1000 years, so it's possible that each creation day lasted 1000 years.

"For yourselves know perfectly that the day of the Lord so cometh as a thief in the night" (1 Thess 5:2).

"And they lived and reigned with Christ a thousand years" (Rev 20:4).

Before our Father returns for His final Judgment Day, Jesus will reign on earth for 1000 years — the millennium — the Lord's Day. When Jesus returns, He will lift the veil from our eyes, and everyone will instantly remember everything that has happened since our creation in the first earth age.

Everyone, including John Calvin, will then know the correct definition of the word replenish. These 1000 years will still be a time of salvation. It will be a period of teaching discipline to those who did not overcome in the flesh age. Those who overcome will reign as kings and priests with Jesus during these 1000 years.

God rested on the seventh day. Then, on the eighth day, He formed Adam from the dust and Eve from Adam's rib. He placed them both in the Garden of Eden. God formed Adam and Eve so that Jesus could be born through their bloodline.

"And the Lord God formed man of the dust of the ground, and breathed into his nostrils the breath of life; and man became a living soul. And the Lord God planted a garden eastward in Eden; and there he put the man whom he had formed. And out of the ground made the Lord God to grow every tree that is pleasant to the sight, and good for food; the tree of life also in the midst of the garden, and the tree of knowledge of good and evil" (Gen 2:7-9).

God created a special garden to protect the bloodline of Jesus. Jesus is the Tree of Life, and Satan is the tree of the knowledge of good and evil.

"And the Lord God caused a deep sleep to fall upon Adam, and he slept: and he took one of his ribs, and closed up the flesh instead thereof; And the rib, which the Lord God had taken from man, made he a woman, and brought her unto the man" (Gen 2:21-22).

"And the woman said unto the serpent, We may eat of the fruit of the trees of the garden: But of the fruit of the tree which is in the midst of the garden, God hath said, Ye shall not eat of it, neither shall ye touch it, lest ye die" (Gen 3:2, 3).

Touch - Strong's H5060 - to touch, lay the hand upon for any purpose, and to lie with a woman.

"And the eyes of them both were opened, and they knew that they were naked; and they sewed fig leaves together, and made themselves aprons" (Gen 3:7).

Many people are surprised to learn that the word apple isn't in the Bible. There were many fruit trees in the garden, but Adam and Eve did not eat an apple from an apple tree. The tree of the knowledge of good and evil is the wicked serpent, Satan, that old dragon, the Devil himself.

"Thou hast been in Eden, the garden of God" (Ez 28:13).

Father describes Satan as a serpent because his character is one of a rebellious, tricky, low-down, dirty, hissing, deceitful, sly scum of the earth, evil, and deceiving devil.

Satan didn't waste any time getting straight to his mission to deceive and corrupt this special bloodline. By coming to Earth without being born into a flesh body, Satan gave up his ability to enter the kingdom of heaven.

This evil serpent approached Eve and gave her his apple-pie sweet talk, deceiving and tempting her to eat the fruit of the tree. The serpent told Eve that if she ate from the forbidden tree, she wouldn't die. Instead, her eyes would open, and she would become like the gods, knowing good and evil.

Eve believed all the serpent's apple-pie lies. Great desire for the forbidden tree overtook her as she disobeyed God's command and partook of the knowledge. She took of the tree and gave it to her husband Adam, and he also ate.

Then, after eating, their eyes opened, and they realized they were naked. Satan had deceived and seduced them. There was a fig tree nearby, and because of their shame, they sewed fig leaves together and made aprons to cover their private parts.

"But I fear, lest by any means, as the serpent beguiled Eve through his subtlety, so your minds should be corrupted from the simplicity that is in Christ" (2 Cor 11:3).

Beguiled - Strong's G1818 - to seduce wholly, beguile, deceive.

Wholly seduce means to utterly and completely seduce.

To touch means "to lie with a woman." Beguiled means "to seduce wholly." Satan himself, being a handsome angel, approached Eve and fully seduced her verbally, mentally, emotionally, and romantically. Satan was in the Garden, trying to destroy the bloodline through which Jesus was to come.

"And I will put enmity between thee and the woman, and between thy seed and her seed; it shall bruise thy head, and thou shalt bruise his heel" (Gen 3:15).

God placed enmity, or hatred, between Satan's seed — his children — and Eve's seed. Eve's seed is Jesus and those who love Him. We will bruise Satan's head, and Satan's seed will bruise Jesus' heel. Satan's children fulfilled this part of the prophecy when they nailed Jesus' heels to the cross. All who follow Jesus are the bruisers:

"For the ships of Chittim shall come against him" (Dan 11:30).

Chittim - Gr. Strong's - Bruisers. We shall bruise Satan's head.

Father punished Adam, and now, he had to work hard, with sweat on his brow, tilling the ground for food. To make matters worse, his land would now contain weeds — evil tares — thorns, and thistles, making his planting, growing, and harvesting miserable.

Eve's punishment was that her desire would be for her husband; he would rule over her, and she would experience greater sorrow and pain related to her conception and childbirth:

"Unto the woman he said, I will greatly multiply thy sorrow and thy conception; in sorrow thou shalt bring forth children; and thy desire shall be to thy husband, and he shall rule over thee" (Gen 3:16).

The word children is plural here, meaning more than one child. The Garden had a bunch of: apple-pie sweet talk;

touching — to lie with a woman; beguiling — to seduce wholly; realizing that they are naked; covering their naked private parts with fig leaves in shame for what they had done; Eve's seed and Satan's seed will hate each other; and Eve now would have much sorrow in the conception and childbirth of her children. Oofta bangers! What on earth is next?

~ One Bad Apple ~

"And Adam knew Eve his wife; and she conceived, and bare Cain, and said, I have gotten a man from the Lord. And she again bare his brother Abel. And Abel was a keeper of sheep, but Cain was a tiller of the ground" (Gen 4:1, 2).

Again - Strong's H3254 - to continue to do a thing.

After giving birth to Cain, Eve continued in labor. "Again bare" means she gave birth again, resulting in twins. There's no second knowing — intercourse — or conception mentioned here. What happened in the garden involved private parts, nakedness, and conceiving, which resulted in the twins, Cain and Abel, having different fathers. Cain is Satan's seed, and his children are the Kenites, who in future generations fulfilled the prophecy and bruised Jesus' heel as they nailed Him to the cross.

Cain became a farmer of crops, and Abel became a shepherd of sheep. When the teenage boys reached the age where they were required to bring an offering to God to thank Him for all His blessings, both boys simultaneously brought some of their possessions and presented their offerings to God.

Abel had a loving heart. He brought the best of his flocks, showing his gratitude and his desire to please our Father.

Father was pleased with Abel's offering and blessed him because his heart, thoughts, and actions were righteous.

Cain had a heart that was angry, rebellious, conniving, deceitful, and hateful. He didn't bring the best from his fields. Instead, he quickly grabbed some rotten apples for his offering, showing no concern for offering his best or for being thankful and pleasing to God. Father did not accept Cain's offering and didn't even acknowledge it. He didn't bless Cain because He knew that Cain's heart, thoughts, and deeds were evil.

Cain became outraged that Abel had received a blessing while he had not. He cunningly gave Abel some apple-pie sweet talk and convinced him to go into the field with him. Then, in a premeditated and cold-hearted murder, he killed his half-brother Abel.

Cain, having a supernatural father, was a large, hybrid baby, which caused Eve much pain and sorrow during childbirth. Her sorrow deepened when this evil and malicious child killed her loving son, Abel. The inherited sorrow from Eve giving birth to Cain was that there would now be generations of lying, malicious, murderous, evil children living among her good children, bringing them immense sorrow, agony, and suffering.

Adam received real, physical weeds and thistles as his punishment. These weeds are symbolic, and Father gave them to him as a reminder of the true tares — the real evil children now mixed among the good wheat — the good children. Generations of lying, murderous, evil, malicious, rotten children resulted from Eve touching and being beguiled by Satan — producing the rotten baby Cain.

God cursed the earth so that it would no longer produce crops for Cain. He could no longer be a farmer. If he or his children ever grew food, it would have to be artificial or genetically modified. God also cursed Cain to be a wanderer and a vagabond on the earth. Adam and Eve were angry with Cain for killing their beloved son Abel. Just seeing Cain in their presence every day, with his malicious and murderous demeanor, kept their grief and heartache fresh.

Cain moved to the land of Nod, found a wife, and had children with her. He built a city, but because his heart was so evil and murderous, it's likely the people of Nod didn't like him much either. Wherever he went, most people wanted nothing to do with his rotten apples.

Cain's descendants are the Kenites. Since crops didn't grow for them, they likely made their living by raising cattle, mining precious metals, gems, and diamonds, creating jewelry, and engaging in banking, money, and trade. They probably mastered metalworking, producing decorative pieces and idols. They sculpted and sold many items, both large and small, including making and playing musical instruments, and they were involved in entertainment and music.

The words that come out of each person's mouth originate in their heart. Anything that is not good and pure is of the devil. Cain and his children's hearts are evil, so the music and entertainment that the Kenites create have vulgar, rebellious, disrespectful, and murderous connotations and undertones, pumping their filth among God's good children to corrupt them.

For those who feel shocked that Satan has a lineage of children here, why would Satan only send the fallen angels before and after the flood of Noah to impregnate the daughters of Adam? If he sent these angels to destroy the bloodline of Jesus, what would make him so special that he wouldn't do the same thing? He's more evil than those angels. He's their leader.

Jesus told us exactly what happened in the Garden when He was talking to Cain's descendants, the evil scribes and Pharisees. They were the grievous wolves in sheep's clothing who hung Jesus on the cross.

"Ye do the deeds of your father. Then said they to him, We be not born of fornication; we have one Father, even God" (John 8:41).

Fornication, eh? It sounds like Eve was messing around with the wrong "apple tree." Interestingly, these evil liars knew about the fornication that happened in the Garden. They denied they were the children of Satan.

"Ye are of your father the devil, and the lusts of your father ye will do. He was a murderer from the beginning, and abode not in the truth, because there is no truth in him. When he speaketh a lie, he speaketh of his own: for he is a liar, and the father of it" (John 8:44).

Their father was a murderer in the beginning. Cain, progeny of the Wicked One, murdered his half-brother Abel. Satan is a liar, a deceiver, and a murderer. "Of" means a descendant or progeny of.

"Woe unto you! For ye build the sepulchres of the prophets, and your fathers killed them. That the blood of all the prophets, which was shed from the foundation of the world, may be required of this generation; From the blood of Abel unto the blood of Zacharias which perished between the altar and the temple: verily I say unto you, It shall be required of this generation" (Lu 11:47, 50-51).

Jesus was speaking to the scribes and Pharisees, telling them that their forefathers had killed the prophets, including Abel. We know Cain killed Abel. Cain, the child of Satan, was the forefather of these evil people who killed Jesus.

Satan repeatedly tried to destroy the bloodline of Jesus. He did his dirty apple pie tricks in the Garden, and then he had his chip off the ol' rotten block — Cain — kill righteous Abel. Before Noah's flood, Satan sent his angel minions to intermix with the daughters of Adam, giving birth to giants. After the flood, Satan sent another influx of rotten angels to corrupt the bloodline. Jesus explained exactly how these tares became mixed among us in His parable of the wheat and tares:

> Another parable put he forth unto them, saying, The kingdom of heaven is likened unto a man which sowed good seed in his field: But while men slept, his enemy came and sowed tares among the wheat, and went his way. But when the blade was sprung up, and brought forth fruit, then appeared the tares also. So the servants of the householder came and said unto him, Sir, didst not thou sow good seed in thy field? from whence then hath it tares? He said unto them, An enemy hath done this. The servants said unto him, Wilt thou then that we go and gather

> them up? But he said, Nay; lest while ye gather up the tares, ye root up also the wheat with them. Let both grow together until the harvest: and in the time of harvest I will say to the reapers, Gather ye together first the tares, and bind them in bundles to burn them: but gather the wheat into my barn. (Mt 13:24-30)

The good seed is the wheat — the good children. The tares are the wicked children who are not supposed to be here. Being curious, the servants asked, "Where did these tares come from? Shall we do waste removal?" Jesus told His servants no, because the evil ones are tricky and they sometimes resemble the wheat until they grow up into full-grown tares that are evil, conniving, murderous liars.

Sometimes, when the wheat behaves badly, they look like a tare. Satan and his children tempt and corrupt them. Many good children follow Satan's vulgar, rude, malicious, evil, conniving, and murderous behavior. Sometimes, the wheat looks like a tare because of hanging out with the wrong people, who pull them down into the tare's sinkhole for a while.

Jesus said not to pluck them up, not to do waste removal of the tares until His return, because only He knows what is truly in each heart. Until Jesus comes back to decide which people are the evil tares, we are to leave them alone. We don't want to uproot some of the good children while trying to remove Satan's evil children. When Jesus returns, He will cast the tares into the fire and gather the wheat into His barn.

But wait! There's more to the story. Jesus' disciples asked Him to explain the parable about the tares. Jesus goes into detail and now explains to us how these tares got here on Earth — and who their father is. Let's finish the story:

> Then Jesus sent the multitude away, and went into the house: and his disciples came unto him, saying, Declare unto us the parable of the tares of the field. He answered and said unto them, He that soweth the good seed is the Son of man; The field is the world; the good seed are the children of the kingdom; but the tares are the children of the wicked one; The enemy that sowed them is the devil; the harvest is the end of the world; and the reapers are the angels. As therefore the tares are gathered and burned in the fire; so shall it be in the end of this world. (Mt 13:36-40)

Jesus explained His parable to His disciples. Father, Jesus, the Son of Man, created and formed the good seed — the good children — here on Earth, which is the field or the world. He told them that the enemy, the Devil or Satan, planted the evil children. He said that the wheat and the tares are literal children.

Satan planted his son, Cain, in the Garden of Eden. Jesus said to let them both grow together until the harvest, when He will send His reaper angels to bind the wicked children and burn them. Jesus explained to His disciples that the tares were the Kenites, who were the sons of Cain, who was the son of Satan.

"But he answered and said, Every plant, which my heavenly Father hath not planted, shall be rooted up" (Mt 15:13).

"And say, If we had been in the days of our fathers, we would not have been partakers with them in the blood of the prophets. Wherefore ye be witnesses unto yourselves, that ye are the children of them which killed the prophets" (Mt 23:30-31).

These wicked tares accidentally disclosed that their evil forefathers had killed the prophets. They unintentionally admitted that they were descendants of the evil Kenites, who murdered the prophets.

Jesus tells them that they are also serpents and vipers, and that Father will also hold them accountable for all the bloodshed of the prophets:

> Fill ye up then the measure of your fathers. Ye serpents, ye generation of vipers, how can ye escape the damnation of hell? Wherefore, behold, I send unto you prophets, and wise men, and scribes: and some of them ye shall kill and crucify; and some of them shall ye scourge in your synagogues, and persecute them from city to city: That upon you may come all the righteous blood shed upon the earth, from the blood of righteous Abel unto the blood of Zacharias son of Barachias, whom ye slew between the temple and the altar. (Mt 23:32-35)

Cain killed Abel. These are Cain's offspring that Jesus is talking to. He told them that they and their forefathers are responsible for the deaths of all the prophets, dating back to Abel:

> In this the children of God are manifest, and the children of the devil: whosoever doeth not

> righteousness is not of God, neither he that loveth not his brother. For this is the message that ye heard from the beginning, that we should love one another. Not as Cain, who was of that wicked one, and slew his brother. And wherefore slew he him? Because his own works were evil, and his brother's righteous. Marvel not, my brethren if the world hate you. (1 Jn 3:10-13)

The children of the wicked one commit wickedness. Cain was of, or progeny of, the wicked one, the Devil, or Satan. A murderer is evil. Anyone who premeditates murder or takes another person's life is an evil person at heart. Those who love each other and have the love of Jesus in their hearts are righteous.

John Calvin premeditated the murder of Michael Servetus and carried out his evil plan. He delivered Michael to the authorities, knowing they would put him to death.

The evil children of Cain are the Kenites. Just like their father, they hate our Father. They hate Jesus and all Christians who follow Jesus. They killed Jesus, and they will also kill as many Christians as they can:

"When the morning was come, all the chief priests and elders of the people took counsel against Jesus to put him to death" (Mt 27:1).

God had told Satan that his seed would bruise Jesus' heel, and they most definitely did that.

"And I will put enmity between thee and the woman, and between thy seed and her seed; it shall bruise thy head, and thou shalt bruise his heel" (Gen 3:15).

The Kenites bruised Jesus' heel as they nailed Him to the cross. Eve's seed will bruise Satan's head. All of Father's prophecies always come true.

"They answered him, We be Abraham's seed, and were never in bondage to any man: how sayest thou, Ye shall be made free?" (Jn 8:33).

They were lying and pretending to be Abraham's descendants, but they slipped up and said they had never been in bondage. The thirteen tribes of Israel were in bondage in Egypt for over 400 years. These evil tares were not from Israel. These were the Kenite impostors who murdered Jesus.

The Kenites — the children of Cain — infiltrated the Israelites long ago in the Old Testament. They were the scribes hired by the Israelites to copy documents and keep records. Later, they also served as priests, theologians, lawyers, and judges, with extensive knowledge of the law.

"And the families of the scribes which dwelt at Jabez; the Tirathites, the Shimeathites, and Suchathites. These are the Kenites that came of Hemath, the father of the house of Rechab" (1 Chron 2:55).

Kenites - Strong's H7014 - Kajin, the name of the first child, Cain, Kenite(s).

We see here that the children of Cain — the Kenites — finagled their way into the tribes of Israel and became their scribes. The manuscripts needed to be rewritten regularly, and the scribes were those lying, deceiving murderers whom the Israelites hired to copy their manuscripts onto new scrolls. They could write and erase whatever their wicked hearts desired.

These wicked Kenites manipulated their way to the top positions within the priest's office in the temple. When Ezra was leading a large group back with him to Jerusalem to rebuild the temple, he paused for a few days to determine who was with him. When he checked the priests who were with him, take one guess what he found?

"And I gathered them together to the river that runneth to Ahava; and there abode we in tents three days: and I viewed the people, and the priests, and found there none of the sons of Levi" (Ezra 8:15).

It's a downright cryin' shame! There were no priests with him who were of the tribe of Levi. They were all Kenite impostors. When Jesus was here on earth, they called themselves the scribes, Pharisees, and Sadducees. All the priests were supposed to be Levites.

Now we can better understand why the Kenite scribes and Pharisee tares had Jesus put to death. They were the biological children of their father — the Devil — Satan, the evil one, that old serpent who was in the Garden of Eden. They were chips off their ol' daddy imposter's block. Satan had his minions infiltrate positions of preaching, manuscript scribing, and record-keeping. They became theologians, lawyers, judges, and priests.

To see how evil these Kenites are, we only need to read the New Testament and observe what they were doing in the temple with the money, how they mistreated the people, and how they had Jesus crucified.

These grievous wolves in sheep's clothing who were in charge during Jesus' time didn't just magically disappear after they killed Him. Nope, their children are the tares that Jesus referred to in His parable about the wheat and the tares. They will be among us until Jesus sends His reaper angels to harvest the wheat from the tares. They are still mixed among us today, hidden in plain sight, and they'll be doing the same evil things that their fathers were doing in Jesus' day.

Those devious scribes have been changing our Father's Word ever since they started getting their greasy, grubby hands on it, scribing it, and as many other documents as possible to fit their agenda of power and control and to keep people divided and hating one another. They are vulgar deceivers, liars, and murderers, and they use threats, bribery, bullying, blackmail, and bombs to fulfill their horrific greed for money, resources, and control. They are Satan's children, and the works of their father they will do, until Father gathers them up and casts them into the fire.

There are seven churches mentioned in Revelation. Jesus told five of them to repent. Jesus is pleased with only two of the churches. He did not say they had to repent. These two churches taught about how the children of Cain, the Kenites — the tares — the ones who had killed Jesus, had infiltrated into the wheat.

Revelation 2:5 Ephesus is told to repent.

Revelation 2:9 Smyrna teaches about the impostors. Not told to repent.

Revelation 2:16 Pergamos is told to repent.

Revelation 2:22 Thyatira is told to repent.

Revelation 3:3 Sardis is told to repent.

Revelation 3:9 Philadelphia teaches about the impostors. Not told to repent.

Revelation 3:19 Laodiceans are told to repent.

Of the seven churches mentioned in Revelation, Father is pleased with two of them. Seven is symbolic of spiritual completeness. The seven churches represent all Christian churches that claim to follow Jesus. Only a small percentage of these churches had enough oil of truth, repentance, and love in their lamps. We must teach similarly to Smyrna and Philadelphia, as these are the only two Jesus was pleased with and did not tell to repent.

"And when he shall have accomplished to scatter the power of the holy people, all these things shall be finished" (Dan 12:7).

The holy people are Christians. The evil Kenite children are at their father's beck and call, corrupting, lying, cheating, stealing, and killing. We can recognize them by their fruits. Not only did they kill Jesus, but their agenda, their primary goal, is to infiltrate, corrupt, kill, and destroy all Christians as well. Christians are continuously under attack by Satan and his children, who with all their heart, soul, strength, and mind, hate our Heavenly Father — Jesus — and all Christians who follow and worship Him.

These evil tares are the same evil figs that Jeremiah spoke of. They are the evil figs Jesus referred to in His Parable of the Fig Tree. These evil figs hide in the shadows at the tops of every nation worldwide, holding immense power and control across the political, religious, financial, entertainment, and educational sectors globally.

The Kenites have extreme contempt toward all others who are not of their bloodline. They see the world as a stage with them as the puppeteers, deceiving, blackmailing, and bribing all their puppets with their lies. The evil figs use propaganda to trick and manipulate us into helping them gather for themselves complete power and control over all countries, money, and resources. They keep all people poor and have us working so hard to make ends meet that we don't have time to keep up with everything that they are scribing in all of our biblical, historical, and educational books.

Everything these evil scribes write is what they want everyone to believe. Their agenda is to keep people divided and hating each other. All wars and profits from manufacturing weapons are also on their agenda and have resulted in them killing whoever gets in their way in their attempt to own every country's resources and attain global power.

Over the past 6000 years of intermixing, the tares have become worn smooth to be similar in size to the wheat — God's good children. Genetic testing of large, giant-sized corpses that are thousands of years old could provide clues about their descendants by comparing their DNA to that of today. However, such testing wouldn't offer exact proof, as the angels who came to earth after Noah's flood also produced half-supernatural, giant hybrid children. These mixed children also carry a supernatural DNA component.

Kenites and the other hybrids from the fallen angels can choose to love our Father. They are His children, and He wants everyone to follow His path of love. They used to be His sweet little angel children, singing and shouting for joy — before Satan tricked them and corrupted their souls.

~ Apple of His Eye ~

Throughout the history of the Israelites, they have selected their kings from the tribe of Judah. Father prophesied that Jesus would be born and become Israel's King. Satan, aware of this prophecy, used his evil children to attack, corrupt, and infiltrate Judah's bloodline to prevent the birth of Jesus.

The prophecy stated Jesus would sit on the throne of David, meaning He would come from David's lineage. David was part of the tribe of Judah. Another prophecy said that a king or ruler would be born in Bethlehem, which was also in Judah.

For 4000 years, Satan, his evil children, and his angel minions have tried to corrupt the pure bloodline by infiltrating, mating with, and producing mixed children through all of Adam and Eve's generations. They aimed to contaminate the pure bloodline with their blood. Jesus could not have been born with any part of Satan's DNA.

Satan knew that if he prevented Jesus' birth, all souls would perish because Jesus wouldn't be able to sacrifice Himself for our sins. Satan knows from his rebellion against God that his destiny is to be blotted out. In his anger, he wants to take all of God's children down with him to hurt our Father as much as possible.

Satan's first attempt to corrupt the bloodline happened in the Garden of Eden. On at least two occasions, he sent his wicked angels to intermix with and take wives from the daughters of Adam, aiming to destroy the royal bloodline. After his first attempt, God sent Noah's flood to eliminate all the giants that had been born.

Satan was unsuccessful in his many attempts, and Jesus was born through a miraculous conception by the Holy Spirit into the Virgin Mary's womb. After becoming pregnant, Mary married Joseph, a carpenter from Judah. Joseph wasn't Jesus' biological father, so only Mary held the bloodline of Jesus.

"For it is evident that our Lord sprang out of Juda; of which tribe Moses spake nothing concerning priesthood. For he testifieth, Thou art a priest for ever after the order of Melchisedec" (Heb 7:14, 17).

"In the days of Herod, king of Judea, there was a priest named Zechariah, of the division of Abijah. And he had a wife from the daughters of Aaron, and her name was Elizabeth" (Lu 1:5).

"And, behold, thy cousin Elisabeth, she hath also conceived a son in her old age: and this is the sixth month with her, who was called barren" (Lu 1:36).

Jesus was born from the tribe of Judah, the king line, and the tribe of Levi, the priestly line. Mary's parents came from two different tribes. Her father, Heli, was of Judah, and her mother was of Levi. We know Mary was half Levite because her cousin Elizabeth, the mother of John the Baptist, was married to Zechariah, a full-fledged Levitical high priest.

Priests were required to marry a full-blooded Levite woman. Elizabeth's mother and Mary's mother were sisters, and both were full-blooded Levites.

"And Jacob begat Joseph the husband of Mary, of whom was born Jesus, who is called Christ" (Mt 1:16).

Joseph's father is Jacob. He was of Judah and held the legal blood claim to the throne through King David's son, Solomon. Jesus and Joseph had no blood relationship.

"And Jesus himself began to be about thirty years of age, being (as was supposed) the son of Joseph, which was the son of Heli" (Lu 3:23).

(As was supposed) means by law — or in law. Heli, Mary's father, was Joseph's father-in-law. He was of the tribe of Judah and descended from King David's son Nathan.

"The Lord hath sworn, and will not repent, Thou art a priest for ever after the order of Melchizedek" (Ps 110:4).

Prophecy was fulfilled, and Jesus was born a King and High Priest forever after the order of Melchizedek, which means King of Salem — King of Jeru-Salem — or King of Peace. Jesus is our King of Kings, and He is our High Priest.

Abraham gave a tenth of his possessions to Melchizedek. Priests were to receive 10% as tithes and offerings for thanksgiving and the forgiveness of sins. Without priests, there could be no offerings, and thus no forgiveness. Melchizedek brought out bread and wine to Abraham, which symbolize Jesus' body and blood that He shed on the cross for us. Abraham received a blessing and forgiveness for his sins as he gave his tithes to Melchizedek, our High Priest.

Jesus — our King and High Priest — offered Himself as a sacrifice to pay for our sins. He is the Apple of our Father's eye and the only worthy Lamb. Now, we can receive forgiveness when we call upon Jesus' body that He sacrificed for us. After His crucifixion, Jesus went to the spirits in prison, or to those on the bad side of the impassable gulf that exists in heaven, to extend His sacrifice to them as well.

Anyone can choose to love Jesus at any time. We need Him as our Savior to face our Father's wrath on Judgment Day. Contrary to Calvin, we do not have to be one of God's predestined elect to give our lives to Jesus.

"According as he hath chosen us in him before the foundation of the world" (Eph 1:4).

Foundation refers to the laying down of a new base, but it also carries a more catastrophic meaning within the definition.

Foundation - Strong's Heb - a throwing or laying down. G2598 - to cast down, to throw to the ground, to put in a lower place.

The foundation was the destruction of the earth during Satan's overthrow. God chose His elect because of what they did before the casting down of Satan.

The word elect, at the prime, means to try or the tried-and-true ones. God's elect are the first fruits who have proven themselves worthy and have been justified. They are the apples of our Father's eye. They earned their right to be God's elect by standing strong and fighting hard against

Satan before and during his overthrow. Father elected some to be prophets, prophetesses, disciples, preachers, teachers, and any other task He needs them to do. He's the Puppeteer behind it all, using them to accomplish tasks that fulfill His prophecies. Father intervenes in their lives to carry out His plan for the second Earth age.

God used people to ensure that He would be born of Mary. Father will also use His chosen people to stand against Satan when He casts him to the earth as the antichrist. Satan will pretend to be Jesus and will deceive the entire world. Father will use His elect to crush the head of the Serpent — the Old Dragon, the Devil, or Satan.

God's elect have free will to some extent. However, Father uses them to keep His plan on track. He also uses certain people to fulfill the negative aspects of His plan, as shown when He hardened Pharaoh's heart in Egypt, when Cyrus allowed the temple to be rebuilt, and when Esau became one of the two superpowers of the end times. Father forces whatever is necessary to ensure all of His prophecies come true.

Satan cannot do anything unless God permits it. To carry out the negative part of God's plan, Satan will sit in the seat of God, claiming to be Jesus. This massive deception is according to Father's plan to test and prove His children. Who do we love? Father or Satan? Father needs to know who we love and worship, and He will remove those who do not love Him.

Everyone deserves to be born into the generation they are in. The evil, lawless, and rebellious people from the first age were born into the last generation. It's Father's prophecy that wickedness and lawlessness will dominate at the end times, and it takes truly evil people to fulfill that prophecy.

God's elect earned the privilege of living in the final generation. They have proven themselves to be trustworthy servants. They have a duty to fulfill God's prophecy to stand against Satan and allow the Holy Spirit to speak through them — to let the world know that they are worshiping a false Jesus.

"(For the children being not yet born, neither having done any good or evil, that the purpose of God according to election might stand, not of works, but of him that calleth;) It was said unto her, The elder shall serve the younger. As it is written, Jacob have I loved, but Esau have I hated" (Rom 9:11-13).

Before these two babies were even born, God loved Jacob and hated Esau. This reflects the same time as when God told Jeremiah that He knew him before he was in his mother's womb. Before Jacob or Esau did any good or evil in their flesh lives, God elected and chose both children for specific purposes based on what they had done in the first earth age. Jacob remained steadfast for Father, while Esau stood strong for Satan, which caused God to hate him, or more specifically, to hate his behavior. God loves all His children and wishes that everyone will come to repentance.

"I have loved you, saith the Lord. Yet ye say, Wherein hast thou loved us? Was not Esau Jacob's brother? saith the Lord: yet I loved Jacob, And I hated Esau, and laid his mountains and his heritage waste for the dragons of the wilderness" (Mal 1:2-3).

God promised Abraham that his descendants would be as numerous as the stars of heaven and the sand of the sea. Abraham and Sarah had Isaac. Father said Jesus would come through Isaac's seed. Isaac and Rebecca had Jacob and Esau. God said that two nations were in Rebecca's womb, implying that they are two separate and distinct nations. Some theologians believe that Esau, meaning hairy and rough, is Edom, meaning red. They believe Edom is now Rosh, Rus, Rus' land, or Russia. If that's true, then the thirteen tribes of Israel and Russia are cousins.

Father promised that the Messiah would come through Jacob. Jacob had twelve sons. His second youngest son was Joseph, who had two sons, Ephraim and Manasseh. Joseph divided his inheritance, giving half to each son. As a result, there are now thirteen tribes of Israel. God scattered them, and they are now called the Lost Tribes.

Most of Isaac's sons have forgotten their true identity. One scholar, E. Raymond Capt, has traced Isaac's sons as they migrated across the Caucasus Mountains, which led to them being referred to as Caucasians. He showed how they migrated into Europe and Great Britain, and later, many moved into Canada and the Americas. Scholars have identified one tribe by what they called themselves. Initially, they were called Isaac's sons; later, they shortened it to I-Sac's sons, and then to I-Saxons. In the end, they became known as the Anglo-Saxons.

Some scholars suggest that America is Ephraim and Manasseh. Ephraim means fruitful or double increase. Manasseh means to forget, as in making someone forget, or as God has made me forget. The 13 tribes are followers of Christ. America is a Christian nation, and its motto is: "In

God we trust." There were 13 original colonies, and the American flag features 13 stripes. Where each tribe ended up isn't as important as the fact that they have forgotten who they are. However, God has not lost them and continues to keep all His promises.

The Christian Puritans in the 17th century named the town of Salem, Massachusetts, after Jerusalem. They wanted to create a utopian society of peace. As they tried to hold on to their roots and escape persecution in Europe, they established a new Jerusalem in America where they could settle and find safety.

Father loves all His children very much. He created each person exactly as He intended. When He created all the ethnicities on the sixth day, He saw that they were all very good. Many children from every nation stood strong for our Heavenly Father when Satan rebelled in the first Earth age. Father has predestined every group of people to be exactly where they are to fulfill His plan.

Everyone, whether they have received the written law, will be judged based on whether they follow Father's innate knowledge and instincts of right and wrong. Everyone will be judged by whether they are following our Father's path of love.

Anyone who doesn't know about Jesus, or anyone whom John Calvin has told they can't accept Jesus into their heart, will still have 1000 years in their spiritual body, with full recollection, to accept Jesus as their Savior. Our Father is so loving. He will give everyone every opportunity to be saved from His wrath on Judgment Day.

John Calvin taught that only a small percentage of people are God's elect. He said that only God's elect will inherit eternal life. God's elect fought hard against Satan during his rebellion, and Father predestined them to perform essential tasks for Him. However, everyone has free will, and Jesus said, "Whosoever will" shall have eternal life.

"And so all Israel shall be saved: as it is written, There shall come out of Sion the Deliverer, and shall turn away ungodliness from Jacob: For this is my covenant unto them, when I shall take away their sins" (Rom 11:26-27).

Who is Israel? Who exactly is Abraham's seed? Let's find out:

"There is neither Jew nor Greek, there is neither bond nor free, there is neither male nor female: for ye are all one in Christ Jesus. And if ye be Christ's, then are ye Abraham's seed, and heirs according to the promise" (Gal 3:28-29).

If we are followers of Jesus, then we are Abraham's seed and heirs to the promise of salvation and His inheritance. Jesus was the seed of Abraham, Isaac, and Jacob. When we graft ourselves into Jesus, we become His son or daughter, making us blood relatives. We then become children of the promise.

All children of Jesus can claim His inheritance. It doesn't matter what tribe or ethnicity a person belongs to; if we have Jesus in our hearts, then we are His son or daughter and are the children of Israel and Abraham's seed. With Jesus in our hearts, we are the apple of our Father's eye.

~ Poisoned Apples ~

All parents expect their children to follow the rules. When a child disobeys, they receive punishment. The parent makes them apologize and advises them on how to make better choices in the future. Over time, the child must show that they won't repeat their mistake, so that the parents can trust them again.

The entire world is Father's house, and we are His children. Father sent us a letter with His House Rules, explaining how He wants us to behave. He expects us to apologize when we disobey His rules or hurt His other children.

Father doesn't want us to lie, cheat, steal, murder, or mistreat our brothers and sisters. He said to be good little children. He told us He loves us and wishes that we love Him too. All parents want a loving and respectful relationship with their children.

Poppa has feelings just like we do. He told us to worship only Him. When He sees us disobeying His House Rules and worshiping people and things of this world, He feels sad, offended, and hurt. Many people are vulgar, perverted, and follow the ways of Satan. They are not obeying, loving, or visiting Poppa, and they don't even read the love letter He sent to us. Father feels hurt when His children don't even think about Him, even though He has given us everything we need.

Many of Father's children have eaten the poisoned apples. Some churches teach that all people need to do to enter heaven is to repent, believe that Jesus is the Son of God, and be baptized. They are told, "Once saved, always saved." The churches give them a free ticket to heaven and don't teach that being a Christian also requires a lifestyle change.

Being a Christian means being a Christ-man or Christ-woman. It is choosing a clean lifestyle and giving up sin. When inviting Jesus into our hearts, we give Him the steering wheel of our lives. We strive to be perfect and to please Father by doing good.

We must repent and ask forgiveness whenever we mess up or disobey. Father records everything in His Heavenly Book. The only way to erase the wrongs written is through repentance and telling Father — and others — that we are sorry.

"And I saw the dead, small and great, stand before God; and the books were opened: and another book was opened, which is the book of life: and the dead were judged out of those things which were written in the books, according to their works. ... and they were judged every man according to their works. And whosoever was not found written in the book of life was cast into the lake of fire" (Rev 20:12-13, 15).

"For the Son of man shall come in the glory of his Father with his angels; and then he shall reward every man according to his works" (Mt 16:27).

It's important that our name is in the Book of Life and that only good things are behind our name so that we can receive many blessings.

We can't be fake Christians — chasing after all the things of Satan — having both feet plunged into the things of this world seven days a week and only dipping our pinky toe into church on Sunday. We can't sit on the fence. Satan owns the fence. To be written in the Book of Life, we must truly love Father and circumcise our hearts to one that continually seeks to please Him.

We are to love Poppa more than we love our earthly father and mother. We should always strive to be obedient to Him. Loving Father means hating His enemy, Satan, along with all his filth, vulgarity, and perversion that he uses to corrupt and destroy our brothers and sisters.

Father is Immanuel — which means God with us. He was born as Jesus in a flesh body and died for the sins we repent of. If we don't have a clean slate, we'll want to attain that, with sincere apologies before Judgment Day. When we face our Father, it will be much less embarrassing to approach Him without sin.

Apologies are how we receive forgiveness, both from our Father and from others. A one-time apology given at the time of accepting Jesus doesn't cut the mustard. We must apologize every time we mess up. It's foolish to think we can apologize to someone only once early in life and then keep hurting them, believing that one apology is enough. Imagine us being five years old and being mean to our sister. We apologized to her for hurting her, but then, the next month, we were mean to her again. Our sister felt sad again. It only makes sense for us to apologize and ask for forgiveness again.

Father also expects an apology every time we break His House Rules or hurt His other children. Jesus did not say, "Repent once, be baptized, and live as filthy as you please without giving two hoots how I feel about it."

When Jesus returns, will we be able to run to Him and give Him a big hug, or will He say to us, "I never knew you?" We must desire a relationship with Him, strive to love and please Him, talk to Him, apologize to Him, and care about His feelings. If we sit on the fence, Jesus does not know us. At His arrival, we will cry and feel very embarrassed, so much so that we will wish for the mountains to fall upon us.

"Out of the same mouth proceedeth blessing and cursing. My brethren, these things ought not so to be" (Jas 3:10).

There will be no cursing, vulgar, or perverted people in heaven. Heaven will have no one who lies, cheats, steals, or murders. Nobody in heaven frivolously breaks Father's House Rules. We must aim to become the person who will be in heaven, striving daily to be more loving and good.

Those of us who love Poppa want His Heavenly Ever After to come soon so we can live forever with Him. Father says we should strive to be perfect. To love Him is to follow how Jesus showed us. He is the Way, the Truth, and the Life.

"Be ye therefore perfect, even as your Father which is in heaven is perfect" (Mt 5:48).

We feel embarrassed when we mess up, knowing that Jesus is right here beside us. His presence surrounds us. He knows every thought, hears every word, and sees every action that we do. We keep our slate clean, repenting for every blunder — telling Him we're sorry, asking for forgiveness, and requesting His help to do better.

"But as he which hath called you is holy, so be ye holy in all manner of conversation; Because it is written, Be ye holy; for I am holy. And if ye call on the Father, who without respect of persons judgeth according to every man's work, pass the time of your sojourning here in fear" (1 Pet 1:15-17).

"And to her was granted that she should be arrayed in fine linen, clean and white: for the fine linen is the righteousness of saints" (Rev 19:8).

The more righteous acts we perform, the more beautiful fine linen clothing we will receive from Father. Some people won't have many garments to wear because, written behind their name in the Heavenly Book, they don't have many righteous acts. They are the basic kids who will wear basic clothing in heaven.

"He that overcometh, the same shall be clothed in white raiment; and I will not blot out his name out of the book of life, but I will confess his name before my Father, and before his angels" (Rev 3:5).

Some people will have their names blotted out of the Book of Life.

Judgment Day is payday. When Father opens the books, He will see everything written behind our names. Those who have performed many righteous acts will receive many rewards, blessings, and fine linen garments.

Payday is an exciting day to look forward to. Being by His side forever, we will enjoy all of His magical Heavenly rewards and blessings that He has in store for us. To me, it is like being a little kid who can't wait for Christmas morning to arrive.

For those who don't give two hoots about Father, payday will not be an enjoyable day. All disobedient, evil, vulgar, perverted, and filthy-minded people will turn to ashes — just like Satan will.

Before Judgment Day, Jesus will reign on the earth for 1000 years. All overcomers will have their destinies secured forever. The first death is the death of the flesh. The second death is the death of the soul. Those who overcome before Jesus returns will never again have to worry about the death of their soul during those 1000 years. They have overcome. It's a done deal.

"Blessed and holy is he that hath part in the first resurrection: on such the second death hath no power, but they shall be priests of God and of Christ, and shall reign with him a thousand years" (Rev 20:6).

"And hath made us kings and priests unto God and his Father; to him be glory and dominion for ever and ever. Amen" (Rev 1:6).

The overcomers will reign as priests and kings with Jesus, and He will give them a golden ticket to heaven. Their role is to serve the people, teach the sheep, and bring them into the fold of the Good Shepherd.

Those who don't overcome will be thankful that those 1000 years remain a time of salvation. The overcomers will teach them discipline and how to get their act together. Those hard-hearted people will become quite malleable to work with after they experience extreme embarrassment and shame when Jesus arrives. They are who they are — who they are — who they are. Many people will definitely need the entire 1000 years to discipline themselves.

"To him that overcometh will I grant to sit with me in my throne, even as I also overcame, and I am set down with my Father in his throne" (Rev 3:21).

Strive diligently to overcome and live a life filled with love and kindness. The desire to love and please our Heavenly Father comes from deep within each person's heart. We must love the Lord our God with all our heart, soul, strength, and mind, and love our neighbor as we love ourselves, to be granted entry into the mansions of heaven. We will all reap the blessings — or the consequences — of our choices.

The Israelites had to wander in the wilderness for forty years. Father said the reason for this was to humble them and to prove them. None of the original people who left Egypt could enter the promised land of Canaan, as they didn't cut the mustard. Only their children entered the land of milk and honey.

"And thou shalt remember all the way which the Lord thy God led thee these forty years in the wilderness, to humble thee, and to prove thee, to know what was in thine heart, whether thou wouldest keep his commandments, or no" (Deut 8:2).

We can't enter the Promised Land of heaven unless we are humble and become like little children. We must desire a Poppa-child relationship, loving and trusting Him. Father is testing and proving us to see whether we will love Him or Satan, and if we will follow His House Rules or not.

"And said, Verily I say unto you, Except ye be converted, and become as little children, ye shall not enter into the kingdom of heaven. Whosoever therefore shall humble himself as this little child, the same is greatest in the kingdom of heaven" (Mt 18:3-4).

Father's servants desire what He desires. We hope everyone will choose His path of love. We must stop eating Satan's poisoned apples. Indulging in and promoting sinful, vulgar, and perverted things is the opposite of what Father desires. He said, "Be ye holy, for I am holy."

Many churches teach, "Jesus loves us just as we are." Some say, "We all sin, and that's just the way it is." Others say, "God loves us all, sin and all." They enjoy eating these poisoned apples because they love their life of sin. They believe they can continue in their sins and still enter the pearly gates of heaven.

Do you remember the story of the 10 virgins and how Jesus told five of them, "I never knew you?" Those five had eaten poisoned apples, and they didn't have enough truth, love, and repentance in their lamps. We will either hate sin and run from it, or we will sit on the fence, with one foot in the world and believing that the other foot will slide us into heaven. To enter heaven, both feet must be entirely on Father's side of the fence. Otherwise, we may not enter the marriage supper of the Lamb.

"Pure religion and undefiled before God and the Father is this, To visit the fatherless and widows in their affliction, and to keep himself unspotted from the world" (Jas 1:27).

Servants must go among sinful people to teach them about Jesus. While we are with them, we should continue acting as Christians. In Sodom and Gomorrah, Lot's righteous heart was vexed daily because the people were committing abominable acts of unrighteousness.

We have to work in the muddy field, but we have to leave judgment up to Father. Nobody knows whose heart or mind Poppa is pricking. We don't know if we are being used as the original seed planter or if Father is using us to water someone else's seed. It's not our business. Our business is the same as Lot's business, and that is being a worker in Father's field. We don't know what is happening behind the scenes. That's Father's business.

As servants, we must be around different sins, filth, and vulgarity. Being a holy Joe who stays away from sinners does nothing to persuade these poisoned children to choose Father's path of love. How can we tell those poisoned children how deeply our Father loves them if we're too holy to go around them?

Our preference is that there would be no evil, perverted, or disobedient children. That day will arrive when all of Satan's poisoned apples will no longer exist. In the final heaven age, we will have our memories erased and won't remember the evil. Father will wipe our minds clean of all hurt and pain. There are no tears in heaven, so that means no memories that will make us sad.

We will have no memory of anyone that Father disposes of. If a family member or loved one follows Satan, it will be as if they never existed. Until that day, as servants, we must work hard to help Father bring His children back to Him. We must show them Father's love, show them that His path is easy, and that it's the only path that gives us complete peace and safety. We must deliver the Doctor's medicine to everyone who has eaten the poisoned apples.

~ Apple-y Ever After ~

Father is every speck of energy that exists, has always existed, and will forever exist. Nobody can create or destroy energy; it can only change form. His energy stretches across the universe, with no beginning and no end. It has simply always been. There's no wall at the edge of the universe, so there's no end to Father's energy. If there were a wall, like all walls, there would have to be something on the other side.

All energy is Father, with intelligence and consciousness. Nothing is separate from Him. He permeates everything. Each little bubble of energy is just a speck of the whole, and the whole is God.

God's energy is everything we can breathe, see, smell, hear, and touch. Everything we can imagine — space, matter, planets, galaxies, stars, all living beings, water, grass, and trees, as well as every particle, molecule, atom, cell, and speck of dust — is all created from God's energy. Father changed His energy into different forms. Using His energy, He also created a spiritual body for Himself.

Father is the owner of all energy. With just a thought, He commands all of His energy particles to take any form He desires. All particles obey instantly, without question. Just like our bodies, when our brain commands, all our joints comply without question. Our bodies are a mass of tiny energy bubbles that have existed forever. Father changed dust energy into flesh, and upon death, the flesh changes back to dust — which is energy. We are smaller than a pinprick compared to Father's enormous, endless energy.

When creating the Earth, Father changed some of His energy into a perfect ball hanging in the universe. Walk carefully on Earth, as we are walking on Father's energy. Be loving when we speak to ourselves and others, because we are talking to Father's energy. Father feels and hears everything. It's imperative that we love one another. Father loves every little particle of energy. We are tiny, special working parts in the spokes of an enormous, well-oiled wheel. We all need to work together for the good of the wheel.

Love is the oil that greases the wheel. If one of His little bubbles of energy has an unfixable glitch, becomes unloving, and oils the wheel with hate, then Father will change our bubble into ashes — which is also energy. To enter Father's Apple-y Ever After, we must choose love. Love our Father, love ourselves, and love others. Love wins every time.

Making mistakes is normal. We have all been disobedient, rebellious, and disrespectful to others. Sometimes we make good choices, and at other times bad ones. Mistakes are important because they help us learn and grow.

When we hurt others, we must apologize to be forgiven. Just one hurtful word or action can turn someone's entire life into a journey of pain. Calling people names or criticizing their appearance may lead to low self-esteem. With a single action or word, we can steal someone's happiness, sometimes forever.

Father said, "Thou shalt not steal," and that also includes stealing happiness from others. The less hurtful we are toward others, the fewer apologies we need to make. We must take responsibility for our actions and apologize to people right away so that the pain we've caused doesn't grow worse.

Anything we don't apologize for in this life will be addressed at the Pearly Gates. Those who refuse to say sorry cannot enter the Golden Gates of Heaven. Father knows everyone's hearts, thoughts, and feelings. Fake apologies are simply non-apologies. Heavenly people choose love and apologize when they hurt others.

Father never damages the Poppa-child relationship. The children damage it by being disobedient to Him, hurting themselves, or hurting others. All people require apologies. Father also requires apologies to Him and to His other children.

After damaging their relationships, many people find it difficult to repair those broken bonds. Even when they try their best, they often cannot restore the relationship to its former state. They feel uneasy being around the person they hurt. The Father-child relationship also becomes uncomfortable for the child out of guilt and shame.

Many children break their relationship with Father through disobedience, rebellion, indifference, and chasing after the cares of the world. They drift away from Him because they feel ashamed to face Him. As a result, Father practices tough love and doesn't rescue them from their difficult situations, allowing them to wallow in their misery.

Father patiently waits, hoping they will return to Him. He is joyful when a child comes back to loving and respecting Him — they now have His full attention. This child is now the apple of Father's eye. If someone pokes one of His precious children, they are poking Father in His eye. They will experience His wrath as He protects this little one who loves Him.

Father knew we would make mistakes and couldn't fix all our broken relationships. Out of His deep love, He gave Himself as the sacrificial Lamb to pay the enormous debt we owe. He became our Savior, our Lord Jesus Christ.

Each child must stand before Father to undergo His interrogation regarding all our words, actions, thoughts, and behaviors, as well as any apologies still owed to Him, ourselves, or others. We cannot enter Father's presence on our own. We would melt away into oblivion out of embarrassment and shame for our filthiness. Father is pure and clean. With Jesus by our side, we can now approach our Father. Jesus will stand before Him as our Mediator — our Lawyer. Jesus will plead our case and will tell Father that He has paid our debt for us.

When Father receives this perfect payment and confirms that we have made sincere apologies, He will no longer see our imperfections. He will stamp us as perfect because Jesus — who is perfect — gave Himself as the sacrifice and paid the punishment we deserve. We must apologize to everyone we've hurt. After every wholehearted effort, whatever remains, Jesus will pay our outstanding debt.

Only love can enter heaven. The children who have learned the art of love are a perfect match made in heaven. Only those who desire and choose Father's path of love will enjoy eternal happiness in heaven — Apple-y Ever After.

~ Little Buddy ~

Imagine that we are Father, and we invented and created many beautiful, high-tech coffee pots. We built them with free will and provided them with an instruction manual outlining our expectations for how we wanted them to behave. Everything is going along great, and we are enjoying robust and delicious coffee every day.

Then, putting a crack into our heart, one Little Buddy coffee pot — out of the blue — decides that he wants to be a disgusting toilet instead of a beautiful, aromatic coffee maker. Little Buddy begins using vulgar language toward us and our other little coffee pots.

We can all imagine what we might say to this little rebellious coffee pot. Maybe something like, "Hey Little Buddy, I created you to make me decadent, aromatic coffee. Instead, you are filling yourself up with vulgar, stinky, and disgusting sludge.

Well! Fiddlesticks, Little Buddy. I have no use for toilets, so I'm gonna go munch on some lunch and give you some time to think about your decision. Hmmm. Maybe after you go through enough cycles of flushing that filthy brown stuff down your pipes, you might decide to come back and make delightful coffee for me once again.

Little Buddy! Seriously! The other little coffee makers are not happy about your stench. You're forcing them to endure an unpleasant odor, so if you don't start making heavenly coffee for me again within a specific time — as I programmed you to do — I'll have to take you apart. That way, my other little coffee pots, who love brewing rich, aromatic coffee, can enjoy their existence without your nasty, repulsive toilet smell lingering around them.

Awwww. I'm sorry, Little Buddy, but I assembled you to dispense delicious, decadent coffee, and if you refuse to do that for me, I'll have to dispose of you! It will be heartbreaking for me to disassemble you because I love you, Little Buddy. I'm sure you can understand that I only want aromatic, delicious-tasting coffee. Your repulsive smell, coming from all those little dilli bobbers floating in your toilet, is ruining everyone else's delightful and heavenly coffee experience. The choice is yours, though, Little Buddy.

Little Buddy, I promise you will be happy being a little coffee pot, producing lovely aromatic tastes and smells. I promise that each time you serve a cup of delicious and robust coffee, every recipient will feel amazing after enjoying the aroma and flavor of your coffee. I promise it will give you great satisfaction.

Aww! Shucks, Little Buddy. I'm being so patient. Please be a good little coffee pot, just as I invented you to be. You know that nobody wants disgusting toilets near their delicious coffee. Whoever told you that a disgusting toilet would be welcome in coffee heaven was lying to you, Little Buddy. Nobody drinks coffee from a toilet.

Aww, Little Buddy. Please read the instruction booklet I gave to all my adorable little coffee pots. It will tell you how to be a happy little coffee pot. I described in the manual how much I love you. I told you the reason I made you. It was so I could enjoy your heavenly coffee. Please, Little Buddy…

Little Buddy??? Little Buddy??? Aww, Little Buddy."

www.ingramcontent.com/pod-product-compliance
Lightning Source LLC
LaVergne TN
LVHW010936110826
845149LV00013B/2622
* 9 7 9 8 9 9 4 6 2 0 0 5 2 *